REVERSING RACISM

REVERSING RACISM

Uche Ekezie

ELM HILL

A Division of
HarperCollins Christian Publishing

www.elmhillbooks.com

Reversing Racism

Published in Nashville, Tennessee, by Elm Hill, an imprint of Thomas Nelson. Elm Hill and Thomas Nelson are registered trademarks of HarperCollins Christian Publishing, Inc.

Elm Hill titles may be purchased in bulk for educational, business, fund-raising, or sales promotional use. For information, please e-mail SpecialMarkets@ThomasNelson.com.

All Scripture quotations, unless otherwise indicated, are taken from the New King James Version®. © 1982 by Thomas Nelson. Used by permission. All rights reserved.

Library of Congress Cataloging-in-Publication Data

Library of Congress Control Number: 2018959520

ISBN 978-1-400306237 (Paperback)
ISBN 978-1-400306244 (eBook)

"If there is no struggle, there is no progress."

FREDERICK DOUGLASS

In loving memory of my late sister Angela Chineme Nwanya (nee Ekezie), a senior researcher with the Nigerian Raw Materials Research and Development Council, who passed away in September 2011 at just age forty-four.
We still miss you dearly big Sis.

Acknowledgement

I appreciate the contributions of my in-house editor, my lovely wife and mother of my three wonderful children, Joy Chiamaka Ekezie, a pediatrician at the Lagos University Teaching Hospital.

CONTENTS

CONTENTS

ABOUT THE BOOK

The resurgence of nationalist movements in the West from 2016 once again pitches populist conservatives who seem bent on preserving their societies' homogeneity and to an extent, way of life, against pluralist liberals more open to the idea of granting increased legitimacy and inclusion to minority groups. Such rounds of debate are not new, as these traditional opposites have been at it for as long as human existence, they just happen to go by varied names in different societies. Whether you choose to call them Conservatives and Liberals or the Right and the Left, it remains the same traditional clash of ideology; *to either maintain the status quo, or accept some potentially disruptive change?* It is said that the only constant thing in life is change, hence regardless of how resolute anti-change proponents may be received; there always comes a time when the momentum of social dynamics makes these changes in every society inevitable. The usual question is for how long the Right in each instance of social unrest can hold out before yielding to the forces of change.

This latest rift has stoked and brought to the fore factional and racial tensions which had for some time been consigned to the background. There are increased reports of racial profiling by law enforcement officers, a general rise in apathy towards immigration and minority groups, and even more open confrontation between both sides of the debate. This is not because the number of race related incidents ever went down and is suddenly on the rise again. On the contrary, the problem never abated; it is just that victims are no longer comfortable accepting discrimination as the norm and are more likely to speak up now more than in the past. This has led to a spike in the number of reports of racism in the last couple of years. The situation is not dissimilar to the flood of disclosures that occurred when sexual harassment allegations were leveled against some major names in the US movie industry, which became known as the *Me-Too Movement* which shook Hollywood in 2017. Additionally, the influence of social media with its wide coverage in shaping public consciousness has literally made anyone with a smart phone a potential news reporter and consumer these days.

Racism has once again become a major subject of public debate and is likely to continue so as societies become more globalized and diverse. The imminent new liberal world order with its message of diversity and inclusion; took root in the aftermath of the Second World War and is likely destined to survive this current resistance by nationalists in Western Europe and more importantly the United States.

This book is written in an effort to tackle what in recent times has become a significant issue and the *elephant in the room* whenever equity is being discussed in diverse multiracial settings, especially as globalization continues as a disruptive force around the world.

The title of the book *Reversing Racism* is not to be confused with *Reverse Racism* or *Reverse Discrimination*; which is retaliatory discrimination perpetrated by minorities as a reaction to racism, and in my opinion, does more to fuel rather than remedy the problem of racism. Targeting hostilities or bias at the generality of a people because of their race cannot be viewed as anything other than Racism, hence Reverse Racism is condescending to the troughs of human behavior that is responsible for Racism to begin with, and I do not encourage it.

It begins, like most books on the subject, by giving the reader a view of the root cause and different expressions of racism. But as you progress, the book provides suggestions on what victims of racism can do on their part to proactively reverse *circumstances* that invite racism.

The intent of this book is not to exacerbate racial tensions; instead it is a call to *positive* action that can roll back the symptoms which perpetuate this scourge with an action plan that aims to reduce the gulf between the "haves" and the "have-nots". It is a gathering of my thoughts on what minorities in the West and people of African descent, as the main victims of racism can do; *not necessarily to* confront racism head on, but to subtly address the traits that encourage racists to behave in the way they do.

It is great to have laws that bar dehumanizing speech in public spaces like the media, but such laws will not stop racists from using obscenities in the privacy of their homes and offices. Prejudices are not innate, but socially acquired, and since such acquisition is predominantly interactive, it is this social discrimination and cognitive prejudice in homes, offices and monoracial discourse that perpetuates racism from generation to generation, conferring it with a status of tradition. To ebb this trend and push it back will be no mean feat, and requires a battle for hearts and minds, that aims at removing those prevailing malignant conditions which racists use as justification for their behavior. This book suggests what colored people can do on our part to etch away at racism, one chunk at a time.

I encourage you to do more than just read this book. Feel free to use a hi-lighter pen to mark sections in the book that may or may not appeal to you in one way or the other. In the end, my hope is that it provides an effective reference for doing your part to roll back racism. It is of course predominantly based on my personal experiences and opinions on the subject; and I by no means claim to be an expert much less a final authority on the matter. So, do not be surprised if we differ considerably on any of the points I have raised. In addition, to better appreciate what these experiences are, the book begins with a little background on myself and incidents that prompted me to choose racism as a subject of the book, before delving into the subject matter in the subsequent chapters.

I have made the book as condensed as possible by not over elaborating on topics. It is a light read in the hope that no reader uses its size as an excuse not to read or benefit from it, as its contents are relevant to all. Its language is simple and easy for the lay as well as the more scholarly to understand. This way every kind of reader can appreciate it, even those who do not like voluminous books can get through it in a day or two. So, please go ahead and enjoy my foray into sensitive waters.

CHAPTER 1

WHY THIS SUBJECT?

The Free World is witnessing another cycle of Racial Activism. In the last century, we have had the likes of the Civil Rights Movement, the American Indian Movement among other Movements aimed at inclusiveness, and most recently we had the Black Lives Matter Movement. These cycles of racial activism are beneficial due to the fact that each time they serve as a reminder of just how far nations that make up the Free World are from the societies of liberty they desire to have. This is not to say that remarkable progress has not been made the entire time. After all it was just seventy years ago that George McLaurin; a fifty-four-year-old African American, received lectures at the University of Oklahoma in an anteroom apart from Caucasian students in 1948; despite the US supreme court ruling which allowed him to attend the institution. Again, it was seven years after in 1955 that the indelible Rosa Parks, then a forty-two-year-old seamstress made her famous stand when she refused to give up her seat on a bus in Montgomery, Alabama. So, we should not fail to acknowledge the progress these cycles of Racial Activism have yielded as well as continue to acknowledge those who led these leaps in civil rights. However, despite these leaps forward, there is still ways to go before we can consider our societies as level playing fields for all ethnicities.

I find it ironic that while these movements go on in the West, there are millions of people in sub-Saharan Africa and other underdeveloped nations, who never having left their homelands, and but for movies and news bulletins about racism are oblivious to the phenomenon. The concept of racism is as foreign to those of them in the heart of Africa as snow, for understandable reasons; they might have heard about it, but a majority of them have never experienced it. It is more often when you move to southern Africa where colonials marred the continent with apartheid history and toward the Arab North of the continent, that you meet blacks who actually have had a personal experience of racism. I am one of those "privileged" black Africans who was fortunate to have his dignity preserved well into adulthood by being shielded from what I see as scourge, and I would like to share how my first experiences and those of my black brothers and sisters have affected my being to the point of writing this book.

As introductions go; first and foremost, I am Nigerian, born and brought up in the most populous city in sub-Saharan Africa – Lagos – current population over twenty million. Lagos is a buzzing metropolis and melting pot of some two hundred and fifty ethnic groups that make up Nigeria. The predominant languages spoken in Lagos are English (the lingua franca in Nigeria), Yoruba (the indigenous language of the state) and Pidgin English (part of a continuum of English Pidgins spoken in West and Central Africa). Born to two civil servants (government employees) and raised in a Roman Catholic home; though today I cannot confidently say I am a confession-going, church-reconciled, practicing Roman Catholic. Why? Well, let us just say I have not been worthy of receiving holy communion at a Catholic church in the tenor so years, that led up to me writing this book – Catholics will understand what that means.

So, continuing with my life's story. When I was old enough, in keeping with the family tradition (a tradition started by my parents who are now late), I proceeded to the University of Nigeria for my first degree in Electrical Engineering. At the University of Nigeria, we had and still have what I consider a very interesting motto which reads: "*To Restore the Dignity of Man*". As an undergraduate, I occasionally wondered what the institutions founders and academics who conceived of this motto had in mind? Why would Mankind need its dignity restored? Could it be because of the horrendous things' mankind had done over the course of history? Maybe treachery to other less privileged human beings and our abuse of the planet perhaps, meant we needed our dignity restored? I would occasionally wrestle with these thoughts and sometimes joked about them with fellow undergrads.

It was not until many years after graduation when I sojourned to various continents that I began to see, and occasionally experience the demeaning treatment colored people and Africans in particular, endured in these parts of the world. It was then I realized what the founders of my first Alma-Mata might have had on their minds when they conceived of this grand mission of restoring Man's dignity. It was not necessarily the dignity of all of humanity they were overly concerned about; after all, how could they hope to impact the dignity of humanity from a little-known university campus in the heart of sub-Saharan Africa? I eventually came to the conclusion that it was more likely the *Dignity of the African Man* they were hoping to restore, and my theory was premised upon the goings on at the time this motto was conceived.

In the 1960's when the university was founded, many anti-colonial and pan-African movements were just at their peak. In addition, many sub-Saharan African nations were breaking free from colonial rule and gaining independence like dominos right across the continent. On the other side of the pond, a wave of racial activism– the Civil Rights Movement – led by Martin Luther King jnr. and the likes of Malcolm X was also taking the United States of America and indeed the free world by storm. It is noteworthy that in spite of the fact that Nigeria was colonized by Britain and most of her post-colonial institutions were replicas of the British, our true beacon of democracy has always been the United States. This may explain why we eventually dumped the British parliamentary system for an American Presidential model. In addition, a decade or so after independence, we switched from the British right-hand steering drive to the more popular American left-hand drive for our vehicles. So, you can understand why scholars in a newly independent state could have been influenced by the civil rights struggles of brothers and sisters across the Atlantic in America as well as in Africa, to the point that they must have adopted as a mission statement; the restoration of the dignity of the African man. However, they decided to shroud it in the more pragmatic and broad statement – *To Restore the Dignity of Man.*

Like a majority of students who studied at the University of Nigeria (because of its location), I am from the Igbo tribe in the South-East region of the country. Igbos historically are an egalitarian people believing in the equality of every man, which would explain why our societies were republican in nature even before the West introduced democracy to Africa and the world. With exception of few communities, in earlier days most of Igbo land did not have monarchs who ruled over a vast number of peoples like our neighboring kingdoms. Majority of our communities were pretty much governed by a council of elders or chiefs and a chief priest or seer not unlike the seers who advised kings in ancient Middle Eastern civilizations. To this day, there are jokes made about how difficult it is to gain consensus amongst Igbos because every Igbo man is literally an authority unto himself – answerable to no man. However, as is normal with even the most egalitarian of societies, a leader emerged from among these councils of elders' *primus inter pares,* but the position was not hereditary back then like it is today. Because of this lack of monarchs, the British Colonials went on to appoint Warrant Chiefs to head clusters of communities; not necessarily to make us *civil* but more to facilitate their very cost-effective governing policy of indirect rule in our part of the country.

At about the time I was penning down my thoughts in this book, a certain African American performer came under heavy criticism for comments which suggested that the docile nature of slaves permitted the trade to thrive, and hence slavery was more of a choice. The backlash reminded me of a tragic, yet resilient story of Igbo slaves at Dunbar creek on St. Simons Island, off the US coast of Georgia in 1803, called the *Igbo Landing*. A white overseer on a plantation, named Roswell King recorded the incident. A group of seventy-five Igbo slaves in chains and on a coastal vessel, *the York* bound for St. Simons, rose in rebellion aboard the ship, drowned their captors and grounded the vessel in Dunbar Creek. As they relished their brief spell of freedom they broke out in song, but realizing their certain fate in a strange land, led by their chief they marched into the marshy waters where most of them drowned in mass suicide, choosing to deny their oppressors the pleasure of avenging the ship's crew. I recounted this story for two reasons; first it lends credence to the proud and egalitarian nature of my people – the Igbo. Secondly, it and similar stories of slave resistance such as the Zumbi led resistance on Quilombo dos Palmares of Brazil, in the 1600s and the Nat Turner led revolt in the US state of Virginia in 1831 on which Nate Parker's "Birth of a Nation" movie was based, show that slavery was anything but a choice.

Half a century after the 1914 British Amalgamation of Northern and Southern Protectorates (two regions with very distinct peoples and customs) into one country – Nigeria –Henry Kissinger, the US Secretary of State in the administrations of Richard Nixon and Gerald Ford, a man believed to be one of the most effective US Secretaries of State of the post-world war II era; had this to say about my people. "Igbos are wandering Jews of West Africa – gifted, aggressive, westernized, at best envied and resented, but mostly despised by their neighbors in the federation." This he said in early 1969, nine years after Nigeria had just gained its independence from Britain and at the height of a separatist civil war between mostly Igbos and the other tribes in the North and West of Nigeria; a war which pitched an ill equipped Biafran (mainly Igbo) army against the Western and Russian backed Nigerian forces. Among the mercenaries who fought in the war, were Egyptian pilots who flew fighter jets for a newly formed fledgling Nigerian Air force.

Although, differing casualty figures were peddled at the end of the conflict, the conservative estimate was that over half a million mostly Igbo civilian lives were lost in that civil war. Surprisingly, most mortalities were not recorded during battles or skirmishes as one would expect but mostly from starvation as the Nigerian side put up sea and air blockades which cut off food supplies via the coast of Biafra and led to death tolls of genocidal proportions. It is possible that because all this was happening round about the height of the cold war, with the United States licking its wounds in Vietnam, the Nigerian civil war (1967 to 1970) did not get the kind of global attention or condemnation that kind of genocide would attract today. Also, I guess the fact that it happened in an African country in the late 1960's did not help either; *Black lives matter* – need I say more?

To give an idea of just how under reported these pogroms were, on May 30, 1969, Bruce Mayrock a twenty-year-old Columbia University student set himself ablaze on the lawn of the United Nation's New York headquarters and eventually died of his burns to protest the genocide being committed against my people at the time. The selfless young man probably did not realize that world powers set their priorities on oil rather than black lives in those days when human rights was still at its infancy. World renowned Nigerian novelist Chinua Achebe (1930 – 2013) an Igbo Professor at my Alma-Mata, wrote his account of the Biafran Cause shortly before his death, titled *"There Was a Country."* He wrote the book from his unique perspective as Secretary of State of the then breakaway Republic of Biafra, and in it gave an account of his efforts on the behest of the then Biafran leader, Dim Chukwuemeka Ojukwu to draw international attention to their struggle for self-determination. Achebe is better known for his book *"Things Fall Apart"*, which is the most widely read book in modern African literature and now exists in 57 translations around the world.

Despite the unpleasantness of this portion of our history, it and our pre-colonial culture and traditions form part of my ancestry and hence my identity, giving me a sense of pride and belonging. Today Igbos, not unlike Jews, Indians and Lebanese have a reputation as world travelers. It is in our nature to travel anywhere in search of opportunity. In fact, though I do not have the data to back this, but I am quite confident that you will find an Igbo in nearly every nation of the world. If for some reason, you are unable to find an Igbo in your country, then chances are that you must be lacking opportunities there.

Knowledge of one's ancestry fills a void in every human being, a void associated with shared history and identity. This is a void some African Americans, people of the Caribbean's and black Latin Americans whose ancestors were whisked away forcefully from the continent aboard slave ships, must struggle to fill. Most European, Asian and Latin Americans are able to trace their origins to at least a nation of the world. In the West, when people like me with foreign sounding names and accents get asked *where we are from:* we can at least mention a country, but not so for these brothers and sisters in North and South America. Unlike other ethnic nationalities, they cannot trace their ancestry to any one nation on the African continent. All we can tell is that they are of African descent because of their skin tone. Even their native names that might have helped trace their ancestry were taken from them and traded in for their owners' names.

In a sense their continent betrayed them when their ancestors were left to be taken away as slaves. This *betrayal* should ordinarily cause some people of African descent in the diaspora to harbor ill feelings towards Africans from the continent, especially as we come over to the West and jostle for what really is their *quota* of opportunities, which their ancestors labored and died for over centuries. But amazingly that is far from the case; not only are they not hostile, the majority of African Americans for instance, are very welcoming and hospitable to their immigrant brothers and sisters. Honestly, I personally would not blame the handful of diaspora Africans who may harbor animosity in any way towards their kin from Africa. The kind of things their ancestors endured at the hands of their oppressors; slavery, lynching, segregation and other forms of human rights violations, were truly horrific and in-humane. More so, they had to live in societies in which the majority had convinced everyone (including some blacks) that their skin color was a stigma; a falsehood which many of them still struggle with to this day. This is an ordeal most of us from the mother land never had to experience.

The point here is that a lack of knowledge about one's ancestry can undermine one's psyche and indirectly affect their sense of self-worth. This makes some of these blacks susceptible to abuse and victims of racist behavior. Subconsciously, they may feel that the attitude meted out to them is well-deserved. More so, these subconscious thoughts can cause them to act in negative ways that will attract racist behavior. Every so often, I hear Brits from the British Isles make fun of their American "cousins"; saying they do not have a heritage and are therefore less cultured. What they choose to ignore in saying such things is that they share a common heritage with Americans; whether Irish-American, Anglo-American or Italian-American they share the same heritage as their Irish, English or Italian "cousins" respectively, on the other side of the Atlantic. This cannot be said about African Americans because Africa is by no means a nation; Africa is a wonderfully diverse continent. Without mentioning its size, the linguistic diversity alone is anywhere between 1500 to 2000 languages spoken on the continent. So, I beg to differ with Europeans that say Americans lack heritage, as it is the African Americans who specifically have lost touch with their heritage. They have had to adopt culture that they improvised during the era of slavery as their heritage, which has gone on to form the foundations of a great deal of the music enjoyed world over today. To have managed this in spite of all the in-humane treatment and prejudice they endured for centuries, is in itself a testament to their imbued strength and tenacity.

I am not implying that we do not have our own challenges with prejudice in Africa; like other people we struggle with tribalism, nepotism, xenophobia and religious intolerance and so much more. Nonetheless while these other prejudices may also discriminate blindly without reason, they do not quite view people of other groups with the levels of contempt that racism does; hence racism's status as the worst amongst all forms of discrimination. Sadly, as much as governments and other world bodies have done and continue to do quite a lot in trying to legislate these prejudices away, for instance the United Nations International Convention on the Elimination of All Forms of Racial Discrimination of

1965, racism persists in society, maybe subtler than before but still damaging and dehumanizing.

Most colored people not just Africans can narrate some form of racial discrimination they have experienced, even the most successful of them; this author is not exempt. There are many texts and write-ups out there that focus on these racially demeaning experiences and it is not the intent of this book to dwell on these anomalies of human behavior, rather it is my intention to focus on how we can move forward with the solutions that reverse this ugly behavior. Never-the-less, to help people who may not realize what constitutes racial discrimination, I will recount just one of the subtler and yet unpleasant experiences I had.

In the fall of 2008 while working for a Production Plant in Nigeria, I was required to attend a 3-day meeting with horizontal process managers from our company's other plants in the Europe, Middle East and Africa region. I was the only black person to attend this meeting which was held at a production plant in the outskirts of Warsaw in Poland and this would be my first visit to eastern Europe. For the records the incident and those I had prior to and since this one, have never affected my impression of Pols or Europeans in general. In fact, I had many Polish friends during the almost three years I lived in England while studying for my master's degree. We played footie some evenings and hung out in pubs and clubs at the weekends and to this day; I still have close friends from both east and west Europe.

Back to my story, during a tea break on the first day I asked a blonde lady from the host plant (she must have been in her thirties) if she could point me in the direction of the restrooms. We stepped out of the meeting room unto the production floor and she pointed me to the end of the production hall. I must have walked some three minutes before I got to the restrooms and the conditions were to my surprise far from sanitary as I had to hold my nose while using the convenience. I got back thanked her and returned to my hotel at the end of the day. The next day, I felt the need to use the convenience again and was headed to the lavatories when a guy from the host plant asked why I would want to go that far to use the convenience when there were restrooms right above the room we were having our meetings in. It turns out there were open offices right on top of us with rest rooms of the standards I was accustomed to.

Apparently, this blonde lady did not think the only African in the gathering should share the same convenience as other men in the group. As you would expect this upset me very much and I had an option to share this with the organizers who were quite senior to her, but I thought to myself, *If I shared what she did, I would ruin what had up till then been a very courteous and productive team building exercise by the organizers.* So, I opted to keep the episode to myself and left her to wallow in her ignorance rather than upset the good spirit within the team. This was neither the first nor the last time I would experience discrimination and I am sure non-white readers would be able to relate with my account in one way or the other.

I was in my late twenties the first time I left the African continent to Europe and experienced differential treatment based on the color of my skin, and as much as I had heard about racial discrimination, read books and watched movies about it, experiencing racism first hand as a fully-grown adult was quite disheartening. At that time, I would feel for people of color who were nationals of these countries because they had to live their entire lives enduring this kind of prejudice –some definitely more than others –day in day out. Considering how commonplace these incidents have become in society, some readers may ask, why bother about it? It is not like another book can make any difference? Why write another book about racism? In response, I say this is not just another book of *lamentations* on racism, so ensure you read on to the end.

I see a backlash from mostly whites (and on occasion some privileged blacks) claiming that minorities seem to be exaggerating and blowing this issue of racism out of proportion, and maybe milking the situation by deliberately choosing to continue playing the marginalization card, rather than counting their blessings and getting over past injustices. Especially, considering where we are coming from, and all the progress that has been made, starting with the official end to slave trade in 1813, and a civil war that was fought in the United States for principally the issue of freeing slaves, and up to perhaps the forty-fourth President of the United States, Barack Obama whose election to office embodied the actualization of a civil rights icon's dream of a future America. Hence, these privileged ones feel we should consider it a job done, pat ourselves on the back, declare it mission accomplished – and move on.

Well, in response to that school of thought I would ask the following questions; are people of color still being unfairly treated by law enforcement agents around the world? Are people of color especially young males, still not getting equal opportunity and being discriminated against in employment? Do colored business owners still find it more difficult to access credit compared to white business owners? If the answers to these questions are in the affirmative, and as long as white privilege in countries like the U.S.A and South Africa is yet to evolve into citizen's privilege, then as we say in Africa, it is a bit premature to shout, Uhuru! If any percentage of the colored population in our so called free society still suffer these forms of discrimination based on the color of their skin and not the content of their character, then it is fair to conclude that we cannot declare "El Dorado" just yet.

This problem of racism persists and in so far as racism continues to affect the fundamental human rights and civil liberties of a portion of mankind, its disintegration will continue to be a subject of debate and the mission for activists around the world. Having said that, this book is not (like I have said previously) another exercise in finger pointing at racists and racists institutions, but rather my modest thoughts on the way forward.

In my research, I encountered different erudite classifications or dimensions of racism, for example social dimensions and cognitive dimensions, per Teun A. van Dijk in his essay, *The Role of the Press in the Reproduction of Racism*. Another writer identified four different types of racism.

There's *Subtle racism*—slight snubs or racial micro aggressions based on race. There's also *Colorism* within minority groups in which lighter-skinned people discriminate against their darker-skinned counterparts. *Internalized racism* is an issue as well. It occurs when minorities experience self-hatred because they've taken to heart the ideology that dubs them as inferior. And in the 21st century, claims of *Reverse racism* are growing, whether or not they're valid (Nittle 2017).

Another source, the *Oppression Monitor* also proffers four classifications for racism; two broad classifications with two sub-classifications within each broad one. The first broad classification they referred to as Individual-level racism, under which they grouped *Internalized racism* and *Interpersonal racism*. Internalized racism here includes the self-esteem issues called out by Nittle, as well as acquired racial bias; whether it be against colored people i.e. racism, or against whites, i.e. reverse racism. Interpersonal racism is simply the expression of internalized racial bias in social interaction. The second broad classification was called System-level racism, under which they had *Institutional racism* and *Structural racism*. Institutional racism, as the name infers, occurs within institutions and power systems, and finds expression in unfair policies and discriminatory practices. Structural racism on the other hand, is the compounding effects of social factors like, history, culture and ideology that grants privilege to whites while denying colored people of privilege. We can agree that the Oppression Monitor's four types of racism are in the end meshed, with each having some effect on the other one way or the other.

Hence in line with my promise to keep things simple and unsophisticated, I, for the purposes of this book will classify racism into two broad categories, which are simply the ways I personally experienced racism being expressed in my social interactions. The first category, I have heard a few African Americans refer to as subtle or *Covert* racism, the kind I narrated in my personal encounter, when discrimination is not to one's face. This is the kind that results from *Political Correctness*. The other I call blunt or *Overt* racism. An example is when racist spectators haul derogatory ethnophaulic remarks like racial slur or use mocking gestures towards non-Caucasian athletes in say, European football.

Covert racism is of course more common these days, as Overt racism is frowned upon by society and usually attracts mass condemnation and disciplinary repercussions, at least in most western countries. The story can be a bit different in some parts of the East, as populations are more monoracial and overt racism is still very prevalent. It is a possibility that because these nations in the Middle and Far East are only recently getting free from totalitarian regimes, and so the concept of human rights is gradually beginning to become part of national consciousness in the last few decades.

In the next chapter, I elaborate on these broad classifications of racism, as a foundation for the subsequent chapters which are my thoughts on the way forward to roll back the persistent plague of racism. For readers familiar with the tenets of storytelling, so far, I have tried to present the *set-up* for the rest of the book by laying a foundation which explains to readers that racism persists (despite all efforts to the contrary at discouraging it in the last few centuries), which I hope I have done to good effect. The chapters that follow outline factors that fuel racism or the book's *conflicts,* alongside fixes or *resolutions* to these conflicts; with the hope that we can collectively (both sufferers of racism and empathizers alike) agree on a course of action to reverse the scourge of racism sometime in the not so distant future. So, I encourage you to read on and consider my recommendations as you do so.

CHAPTER 2

COVERT AND OVERT

Intellectuals differ on the origins of the word *Race*, but it seemed to first appear in the English language between the sixteenth and seventeenth centuries, when it was used to denote a category or class of persons.

Race ... is probably borrowed from the Spanish word *Raza*, of uncertain etymology (Smedley 1993:37). *Raza* first appeared in Spanish-language discourses that distinguished Christians of "pure blood," sangre limpia, from persecuted descendants of converted Jews and Muslims (Smedley 1993:38; Fredrickson 2002) ... and had little to do with skin color (Hill 2008).

The concept of "race" itself as an illusion – a social invention – which gives some indication as to why precise definitions of "racism" are never fully adequate... In the late eighteenth-century race became invested with biological connotations, and by the early nineteenth century specific theories of racial types began to emerge in academic and other writings. Many of the ideas associated with genetics and racial differentiation were founded on pseudo-scientific theories that are now discredited (Whitehead et al 2013).

ReviseSociology, a blog, defines Race itself as, "a specious classification of human beings created by Europeans (whites) which assigns human worth and social status using "white" as the model of humanity and the height of human achievement for the purpose of establishing and maintaining privilege and power." The idea of Race is based on the ideas of white supremacy and white privilege.

Racism is a form of prejudice, not unlike tribalism, religious intolerance and other instances where preconceived opinions that are not based on reason or actual experience are used to make generalizations about a social group of people. Prejudice is defined as an unjustified or incorrect attitude (usually negative) towards an individual based solely on the individual's membership of a social group. For example, a person may hold prejudiced views towards a certain religion or gender, et cetera. When this bias is based on race, this is called Racism. These ideas that assign human worth based on skin tone, have become so engrained in human psyche that we now have people of different races and creeds trying to elevate themselves on this *"scale of whiteness"*, with some willing to go any length to achieve this. Some go as far as using complexion lightening cosmetics, while others feel that by dating and procreating with persons *"higher on the scale"*, they improve their social standing in society and that of their offspring. A certain African American entertainer when asked why he left his African American girlfriend for a Caucasian girlfriend, responded "Because I wanted my children to be as beautiful as possible."

Certain cultures even have social strata systems dating back thousands of years that segregate people based on their ethnicity and skin tone. Hindis in India, for instance, have their Caste system which divides Hindus into four main categories – Brahmins, Kshatriyas, Vaishyas and the Shudras, then there are the Dalits or untouchables (usually dark skinned) who do not even make the cut to be considered a Caste. Indians today will be quick to point out that the Caste system has been phased out and is no longer practiced. This is mostly true in their cities and among their more educated population; however, it is occasionally still relevant in the rural areas where the less enlightened live.

To drive home the irrationality of prejudices and illustrate how racism and prejudices in general get perpetuated through time, I will draw on an experiment once carried out on a group of monkeys. Eight monkeys were put in a room; in the middle of the room was a ladder, leading to a bunch of bananas which hung from a hook on the ceiling. Each time a monkey tried to climb the ladder; all the monkeys were sprayed with freezing cold water, which obviously made them quite miserable. Soon enough, whenever a monkey attempted to climb the ladder, all the other monkeys, not wanting to be sprayed with cold water, set upon him and beat him up. Soon, none of the eight monkeys ever attempted to climb the ladder.

One of the original monkeys was then removed, and a new monkey put in its place. Seeing the bananas and the ladder, he wondered why none of the other monkeys were doing the obvious, and so he immediately began to climb the ladder. All the other monkeys descended upon him and beat him silly and he had no idea why. However, he no longer attempted to climb the ladder. A second original monkey was removed and replaced with a new one. The newcomer again attempted to climb the ladder, but all the other monkeys hammered the crap out of him. This included the previous new monkey, who by this time was grateful that he was not on the receiving end this time. He participated in the beating because all the other monkeys were doing it. However, he had no idea why he was attacking the new monkey. One by one, all the original monkeys were replaced. Eight new monkeys are now in the room. None of them had ever been sprayed with cold water. None of them attempted to climb the ladder. All of them would enthusiastically beat up any new monkey who tried, without having any idea why. That is how discrimination, religious intolerance, racism and ethnic profiling gets learnt and established as culture, becoming acceptable behavior from generation to generation.

Instead of not thinking twice before following traditional norms, religious or negative ethnic stereotyping, it would make sense if we could get our own understanding, to enable us to have an isolated and better-informed perspective on all decisions that govern and determine the way we live our lives and how we perceive others. I say this because a lot of people are racist without even knowing it. I, for the purpose of this book, have chosen to call this behavior *Race based illusory superiority*. In the field of social psychology according to Wikipedia, "*illusory superiority* is a cognitive bias whereby a person overestimates their own qualities and abilities, in relation to the same qualities and abilities of other persons". Examples of this include, when an "A" student accustomed to topping his or her class begins to get pig headed and develops a *know it all attitude* or when an athletic kid gets similar egocentric ideas with regards to a sport he or she is good at. This can happen within any group, monoracial or multiracial and has nothing to do with racism. However, when this sense of superiority is preconceived by a *lighter skin* person, on meeting a *darker skin* person before even social interaction has taken place or vice versa, this I would describe as *Race Based Illusory Superiority* and therefore *Racism*. An example is where a direct report in the work place refuses instructions from a colored line manager or supervisor because of his or her race.

Illusory Superiority is not to be confused with the Latin phrase *Primus inter pares* which means *first among equals*. *Primus inter pares* is used to describe a member of a group who though formally equal to other members of the group is found worthy and emerges as leader of the group. In a parliament, a Prime Minister is considered first among equals and the fact that he or she leads the nation does not prevent him or her from defending executive decisions before the parliament. In a multi-racial group, say a team in a multinational corporation, the team member with leadership qualities who can steer the affairs of the team most effectively typically is *primus inter pares*, regardless of race. When this first among equals position is given based on race – sometimes called White Privilege – this is Racism.

There are many misconceptions about *white privilege,* so I will take this opportunity to elaborate before going forward. "White privilege doesn't mean that "*a white man was hired because he was white.*" It doesn't mean that all whites are privileged. There are many factors that cross racial boundaries that give or take privilege. Nor is white privilege a problem. The problem is that people of color are not given the same privileges, statistically speaking. Our culture is divided by race. This division is fueled by a politicization of racial issues. There are people on the Left and on the Right, that profit from exploiting this tension and from perpetuating false narratives that feed entrenched views of their followers (The Slasher Pastor 2016).

The result is a deepening of divisions along political and racial lines, which causes us to begin viewing race through political lens and, in doing so, adopt all the false narratives from those who profit off the anger that this stirs up. Racial and ethnic divisions are among the most common and enduring features of political life, as they pose a severe challenge to democratic governance in multiracial democracies around the globe.

On January 9, 2018 during a bipartisan meeting with members of the US congress on immigration, the forty-fifth President of the United States of America, Donald J. Trump was accused of referring to African countries as *Shitholes*, an allegation he vehemently denied. A few days later I would listen to an interview on CNN International, in a Trump strong hold in the US state of Georgia, during which a staunch Trump supporter when asked what she felt about the accusation said; "Sometimes we say things in the heat of the moment," and I remember thinking to myself, *I could not agree more.* In fact, I believe we speak our minds most in the heat of the moment. However, in that supposed comment, number forty-five might have spoken the minds of most of the rest world.

The problem is, that most developing countries view the West as culpable in whatever economic or political situations they find themselves in, whether it be through colonialism or interference in their local politics. By unseating and installing governments at their whim; the West has affected the polity in developing countries for good and for bad. Therefore, to hear that the leader of the Free World might be sitting on a moral high stool and referring to Africa as a continent of *shitholes*, not to mention a Prime Minister of Britain using the words *fantastically corrupt* to describe her most populous country, Nigeria – as the former British Prime minister David Cameron did –can understandably be quite exasperating. This is for the simple reason that Europe (and America by extension) are party to crises in Africa and most of the developing world, and therefore should not be quick to put down their former colonies. That being said, we still appreciate Europeans for their concern and their efforts (even if half-hearted sometimes) at helping the developing world, especially Africa. However, in meddling in the affairs of nations, whether it was genuinely in the name of fostering civilization or spreading the gospel: the way the West interfered and continues to interfere in the affairs of the rest of the world, has left very few nations of the world that can boast of not having had some form of military occupation or confrontation with a European nation over the course of their history. I must be quick to point out that, not in all instances was occupation for the primary purpose of fostering civilization or exploitation (depending on which side of the fence you stand), or even both. Occasionally the goal was to protect and preserve displaced and persecuted peoples, as was the case with Israelis in what was then known as Palestine in the years that followed the Second World War and the holocaust. Lest I digress and put myself in the middle of Arab-Palestinian and Zionist imbroglio, my point here is that colored people see the ideological West as partly responsible, if not for their economic woes, most certainly for their political afflictions, hence we prefer that the West leaves us to call ourselves names. Western leaders calling Africa names can only be best described as very poor judgement.

In my travels to certain parts of the world, the displays of racism I experienced which I found most amusing and ironic was that from so called *brown* people who themselves suffer discrimination because of their race and their faith. This kind of racism stems from the description I gave earlier in the chapter where people feel they need to place themselves on a social scale of *whiteness*. This is born out of a need to elevate one's social status by being perceived as *better racially* than someone else lower on the *whiteness* scale. Nowhere did I see this more than in Asia, the Middle East and even parts of North Africa. Here I saw no attempt to disguise racism – it was Blunt. Probably because in the Middle East and as you head east towards and past the Indian subcontinent to the Far East, people do not score points for political correctness like they do in the West.

In the United Arab Emirates for instance, racism can be quite pronounced. Some Emirati business owners are known to exploit the
desperation of immigrant workers from developing countries and go as
far as enslaving them by seizing their international passports and work
papers, making it difficult for such employees to leave their employment
much less the country. These anti-labor practices and human rights violations are well known to the authorities who do nothing about them.
Also, discrimination, not unlike in many parts of the world is palpable on
the streets, for instance hailing a taxi in the upscale Dubai Marina can be
difficult for a black person. This trend continues as you go further east.
In China for instance there are still some establishments (restaurants and
night clubs) who do not admit black people as per policy. It is not that
these are member only establishments where you can refuse admittance
on the grounds of non-membership, I am talking about early twentieth
century style access denial based purely on race and am sure this obtains
in many parts of the world.

As much as I have never experienced (and never hope to experience)
this first hand, I have been in establishments (bars and restaurants) in
Europe where only the stares I received from other patrons and sometimes proprietors let me know I was not welcome. I even got one of such
cold receptions at an Anglican church in the English countryside from
no one else than the ministering reverend. No one had to tell me that
house of God was not welcoming to all of God's creations. I do not even
want to go into the number of unpleasant experiences I have had with
immigrations at numerous airports because of my non-western passport.
I am talking about encounters from France to China to even Pakistan.
However, I would not describe these incidents as outright racism because
they were more of instances of country stereotyping by immigrations.

As much as we cannot deny that government officials are flawed
subjective human beings saddled with the task of securing their nation's
borders, it is difficult to excuse the kind of selective scrutiny they engage
in as being completely free of bias. These officials are custodians of the
gateways to their nations and intentionally or unintentionally can give

visitors the wrong impression about their travel destinations. More specialized trainings and orientation on handling diverse travelers are needed to reduce unpleasant encounters of this nature.

On my numerous visits to North Africa and the Middle East, I was disappointed to observe that black people would very rarely be employed in white collar jobs. The better earners amongst them would most times be employed in trades and other semi-skilled professions, making blacks the poorest earners in these societies. As poor earners, these societies have grown accustomed to expecting blacks not to be able to afford services at certain high-end establishments, like expensive restaurants and pricey retail outlets. On occasions that blacks are seen patronizing such establishments, the assumption most times by the locals is that they are foreigners or at best amongst a very few elite blacks in the country. In these Arab cities, on the few occasions when I dined in proper restaurants, it was not uncommon to meet waiters and servers asking me intrusive rhetorical questions or looking to get a handshake from the *brother* able to patronize their esteemed establishment, something they would not dare with their more Arab looking patrons. It was so disheartening, and I tried to imagine how the local black populace had to live with this their entire lives. Racism is indeed a cankerworm that must be destroyed in the shortest possible time.

There is another equally negative type of prejudice which is the most perplexing because it does not qualify as racism though black people are again the victims. It is the most pointless of prejudices and a result (in my opinion) of centuries of division sowed among blacks; and has come to be known as Black-on-Black Hate. There are typically two dimensions to it, the first is the dichotomy between the more prosperous colored people or those more elevated in society by virtue of their jobs or business concerns, and therefore are less likely to be victims of racism themselves. As mentioned earlier when we dealt with white privilege; there are many factors that cross racial boundaries like class, family structure, and education, et cetera that give or take privilege; so, what we have is prejudice induced due to membership of a privileged class. These classes of colored people discriminate against their less fortunate brothers and sisters, who in their eyes refuse to make something of themselves and choose to continue to remain victims as well as give colored people a bad name.

To a large extent, their grievances can be justified in one way or the other, after all immigrants from Africa arrive and make it in these very same societies. However, you cannot ignore effects of the innate immigrant consciousness that drives most migrants to succeed– the realization that things are not very rosy where you come from and people are looking up to you to succeed, not just for yourself but for them also. What these black achievers fail to realize is that not all colored people are privy to the opportunities that enabled them and their parents to break free of circumstances and better themselves and their families. Institutionalized racism for instance literally makes it less likely for a young black male to be successful in life versus a young black female who is deemed less of a threat by a structurally racist and rigged system. Besides, even if they were privy to the same opportunities as these colored achievers, not everyone in a demography has the same inherent drive to succeed, and this is true regardless of ethnicity or race. So, there is need for more understanding, patience and tolerance and if you like, love towards those less fortunate in society.

The second and more damaging dimension of Black-on-Black Hate is the internal friction within colored communities struggling to eke out an existence, who get caught up in gang related violence, and other socioeconomic violent crimes, also known as Black-on-Black Crime in the United States and other parts of the world. It is a result of centuries of being told," you *are not good enough*" and" there *is something wrong with your kind."*

One of the factors that overlaps with black-on-black crime is economic status. Poverty and crime are correlated, and low-income neighborhoods often see more crime. Black and Hispanic people are more likely to be poor. It's difficult in many circumstances to extricate the effects of race from the effects of poverty (Bump 2017).

Sociologists and criminologists agree that violent crime is a complex socioeconomic phenomenon. Generally speaking, research shows that poor people commit the most crime: According to the Bureau of Justice Statistics, from 2008 through 2012, "persons in poor households at or below the federal poverty level (39.8 per 1,000) had more than double the rate of violent victimization as persons in high-income households (16.9 per 1,000). The overall pattern of poor persons having the highest rates of violent victimization was consistent for both whites and blacks." Maybe the question should be *why are such a large percentage of black people poor?* (Harriot 2017)

A recurring theme in both articles is the link between poverty and crime; in any community where there is high poverty rate, there will be high crime – it is that simple. I was shocked when I came upon stats on poverty levels in the wealthiest nation in the world; a whopping 40 million Americans are said to be living below the poverty line – 12% of the US population. Crime is bound to be rife where you find this kind of gulf in income existing within the same society. This is the case regardless where in the world these societies are located. Hence the key to reducing crime is putting structures in place, to help the less privileged in society to lift themselves out of poverty. Since a disproportionate percentage of colored people find themselves below the poverty line in most societies (not totally of their own making), concerted and deliberate efforts must be made to lift blacks out of poverty. The way to do this in the West is to remove systemic barriers such as Structural and Institutional racism. A perfect example of this is Affirmative Action in the United States. I will be elaborating more on how we can do this in Africa and the developing world in the next chapter.

I realize that recounting these less than cordial racial experiences and interactions in different societies will not be palatable to some if not most readers, and I do not share them with any ill feeling or bitterness. Rather, I am of the school of thought that believes that in order to chart the course for a desired future, you must first learn from the mistakes of the past – and in this case, the present. Can anyone lead effectively without a deep knowledge of history? I seriously doubt it. The intent of being a student of this kind of history should not be to pick on and dwell on these societal anomalies, no! Rather we should learn from them and work towards making them a thing of the past by working towards civility. For instance, at the end of the apartheid era in the Republic of South Africa, that country did not just ignore the wrongs of past decades, no! Instead their leadership instituted the Truth and Reconciliation Commission to allow members of the public to air their grievances with a view to help accelerate the healing process between the majority indigenous population and the minority white and brown population, as opposed to trying to get even for any injustices done during apartheid. The first step toward healing is admitting that an injustice has been done or that a problem exists before setting out to right any wrongs. Psychologists advice against keeping hurts penned up inside as it can be unhealthy and could lead to depression. In the case of injustices and even personal loss, the repercussions of not sharing these grievances can be hate and retribution which we all know, is counter-productive. It is for a similar reason that I have made this effort to narrate these episodes with the hope that it stirs up a kaleidoscope of emotions in readers before we get down to seeking resolution in the remaining chapters of this book.

Having said that, reversing racism will depend heavily on the ability of third-world countries, especially African countries as well as minority communities within the developed world, to get their economies on the track of prosperity and improve standards of living in their communities. This will also ebb the flow of desperate illegal immigrants to foreign countries where they are sometimes exposed to all kinds of human rights violations, maltreatment and unfettered racist abuse. We are agreed that the disproportionately high percentage of minority demographics who find themselves in lower income brackets in different parts of the world and the effect this has on their involvement in crime and other vices means there is a direct link between economic disadvantage and racist ideology. To discourage racist stereotyping and labeling of people of color, there is a need to get a significant portion of colored populations into higher income brackets in both developed and developing economies. This at least begins to reduce cases of discrimination because of economic class.

In the next five chapters, I have presented five areas in which third-world and African countries can begin the arduous task of socioeconomic emancipation, self-reliance and restoration of dignity with their knock-on effect of rolling back racism. I have arranged them in order of importance and of most impact in my humble opinion, but depending on the uniqueness of every society, readers may choose to prioritize them differently. Regardless of how they are prioritized, I see them as a five-point agenda, (if you like) which if implemented simultaneously and judiciously, can do wonders for African nations and the rest of the developing world.

CHAPTER 3

TRADE NOT AID

Jomo Kenyatta an anti-colonial activist and former prime minister of Kenya was quoted as saying,

"When the missionaries arrived, the Africans had the land and the missionaries had the Bible. They taught us how to pray with our eyes closed. When we opened them, they had the land and we had the Bible." It is hard to find a better illustration of the exploitation Africa suffered at the hands of western nations. First, it was slave trade from the mid fifteenth century that provided the western hemisphere free labor to cultivate their farmlands, then later the European apportioning of Africa at the 1884/85 Berlin Conference guaranteed full exploitation by the West which Africa is yet to completely recover from. Africa's crime was apparent lack of military prowess, being simple folk who lived off the land and the water with no knack for exploration or exploitation, and most unfortunate not to have been innovative in the art of warfare. It has been said that there is a confirmed link between innovations for warfare and technological advancement in dominant empires through history. But I digress. Even today the West continues to shortchange Africa in lopsided trade agreements and underpaid taxes by multinational corporations as whistle blowers like the Panama papers and Paradise papers reveal the ways these corporations use offshore secrecy jurisdictions to spirit profits out of the continent without paying their dues.

The Americas did not treat blacks any better either. After Abraham Lincoln's Emancipation Proclamation freed all slaves in 1863, there was no attempt to give them any land (which was the main means of live-lihood in a then Agrarian society) for them to get started on. This was even though they and their ancestors had worked the lands absolutely free for almost two hundred and fifty years as slaves. At the same time however, immigrant peasants who arrived of their own free will from Europe were allocated millions of acres of free lands in the West and Mid-West of America. Yet somehow, those freed blacks were expected to miraculously catch up economically with other migrant ethnicities – a ridiculous fallacy. And where they did try and succeed, they were either systemically or forcefully pushed back down the poverty line. An exam-ple was the Tulsa Race Riots of 1921 where neighborhoods with one of the most affluent African American communities, home to what was then called the Black Wall Street; were looted and burnt by mobs with State support. Some accounts say the blacks were fired upon with helicopters, a massacre if true.

Similar stories of ordeals faced by blacks in Latin America and other multiracial societies abound, but I will not go on to recount them as that is not the intent of this book. It is a global consensus that no one race has suffered more exploitation and stigmatization than the blacks. As easy as it would be to roll over and keep pointing accusing fingers at other races for the predicament of Africans and other minorities globally, I will not take this easy route by joining many of my African brothers and sisters who lay all the blame of Africa's woes on its oppressors and the interests they represent. Blame must be shared by two sides of this injustice; the Exploiters and the Victims. Asides the perpetrators of this exploitation, the victims – African nations – must take some of the blame for the con-tinent's state.

Africa is the repository of at least thirty percent of the most important mineral resources of the world. We have vast fertile and arable lands with the youngest population and hence greater workforce, of any of the continents of the world. We Africans and people of color have at our disposal resources required to dig ourselves out of the economically disadvantaged positions we find ourselves in globally. Until we people of color stop allowing ourselves to be portrayed as disadvantaged people who continually depend on aid whether it be UN aid to crisis zones in Africa or social welfare in developed countries, the rest of the world will continue to use this as an excuse to look down on the less developed nations of the world. If one took a hard look at the aid from global bodies like the UN these days, it is evident that donor nations have gradually begun to lose enthusiasm and have started developing donor fatigue; and who would blame them? Aid is not a sustainable model for development in the first place; it is an unhealthy set-up which is bad for both the giver and the receiver. People of color need to rise in more numbers to be counted amongst the wealthy people and nations of the world and breathe life into the *Africa beyond aid* slogan.

I am Christian, but I must be honest, one of the factors holding back Africans in particular, and colored people in general is religion. Religion has played a major role in holding Africa back economically today, but this in my opinion is not what Religion is intended for. Agreed, in the past religion may have been used by the oppressors of Africans to numb them to the effects of exploitation. It may have been used by slave owners to quell dissent among slaves and it may have been used by colonialists to make the societies they governed docile and less likely to revolt against foreign rule, therefore making them more likely to keep hoping for divine intervention into their situation rather than organize any form of resistance.

Today, it is my opinion that Africa suffers from religion in a more self-inflicted way. Many Pentecostal and Evangelical Ministers these days are feeding their congregations the Prosperity Gospel and focusing less on the message of salvation, to the detriment of these people. A good number of them are now caught up delivering messages of instant success because of the crowds it draws, but unknown to them; it is breeding a generation of believers hooked on instant riches, immediate gratification and effortless breakthroughs. When religious leaders invoke the name of God, the people are captivated, and not everyone has the ability to question doctrine once it is coming from "respectable men of God." So, when they are unfortunate to be spell bound by men of God with personal agenda, who promise success and breakthroughs in return for tithes and *seeds* sown, they lose their God-given abilities to interrogate the scriptures and discern teachings for themselves and thereby realize the part they need to play for their own success. Prosperity preachers need to be reeled in and discouraged from misleading their congregations because of the influence they possess. Men of God should use their influence to encourage people to get an understanding of how things work; principles that add value to the community, such as creativity, entrepreneurship, dedication, perseverance and responsibility. We need to stop hoping for divine intervention when we have the means to start solving our problems ourselves, while trusting The Almighty for His blessing on our endeavors.

African and colored communities need to nurture creativity, innovation and good governance and the church needs to play a major part in this. Agreed, these are things our governments ordinarily ought to do, but we can help ourselves more; it is the humane thing to do. Success stories of unexplainable sudden wealth should not be the only ones celebrated in church the way they are today, rather people who have succeeded through hard work and perseverance should also be celebrated. Churches should start preaching the gospel of hard work, diligence, productivity, planning, critical thinking, strategy, visibility plans, system building, market and customer analysis, and the processes involved in production of goods and services. Look at colored communities, churches are full of people praying and yet there is so much poverty. Prayer is not the only prerequisite for success, strategic decision-making leads to success. It is possible to be full of the Holy Spirit and still be ignorant of ways to create true wealth. The wealthy and clean cities refugees' risk treacherous journeys to migrate to were not built by miracles; they were built by hard work. It is called "Working the Word (the Bible)." True religion and true Christianity *must* aim to produce productive people. The prosperity gospel is doing more harm than good to Africa.

The difference between the poor and wealthy nations of the world is not the age of their civilization; otherwise civilizations like the Egyptian and the Indus valley civilizations with thousands of years of history would be among the super powers of the world. Canada and Australia for instance, which two hundred years back were budding nations are developed economies today. The difference is not dependent either on endowment of natural resources. Japan with its challenging geography, eighty percent mountainous terrain, unsuitable for agriculture, but is the third or fourth largest economy in the world. Japan is the lead economy in Asia and like other advanced economies such as Germany, the United States, and more recently China, they have shifted from a mostly manufacturing base to a service based, high-tech innovative economy, thereby leaving bulk manufacturing to the likes of China and South Korea. Another example is Switzerland; it does not grow cocoa but produces the best chocolates in the world. In her small territory, she rears animals and cultivates the land only four months in a year, nevertheless manufactures the best dairy products.

Another point worthy of note is that, Professionals from wealthy countries who interact with their counterparts from less well-off nations show no differences in intellect. Racial differences also do not evince importance as migrants who cannot secure work or flex entrepreneurial muscle in their home countries are somehow productive in wealthy developed nations. So, what then is the difference? The difference in my opinion is the attitude of the people, molded over centuries by value systems handed down generationally via formal and informal education to become culture.

When we analyze the value systems of people from developed nations, we observe that a majority value some common principles such as, ethics, integrity, discipline, respect for the rule of law, mutual respect for fellow citizens, love for work and productivity, frugality with finances as opposed to spendthrift, patriotism and punctuality. In less developed nations and many Africans are guilty of this, there is an influential minority that get by without these basic principles in their lives. Unfortunately, this minority for some strange reason are predominantly leaders in their communities. We are not poor because we lack natural resources or because nature has been cruel towards us, we are poor because some of us lack the right attitude. Also, educational systems in some countries are partly responsible for this as students are not taught these principles enough compared to developed societies that have had this enshrined in their value system for centuries. An educational curriculum that does not adequately encourage creativity, innovation and entrepreneurship among students should be revised. Curricula can get overly theoretical due to limited funding for school workshops and laboratories.

We should note that entrepreneurship does not come easy in African society because there are many barriers to doing business such as poor infrastructure, inaccessibility to funding for startups and a general lack of incentives. There is not enough government intervention in the business environment to protect national companies and the idea of Trade Wars to protect local business is foreign to us in Africa. By and large our institutions and societies are almost designed to churn out more workers and not enough entrepreneurs.

It is a hard pill to swallow but Africa more than the rest of the world is responsible for the situation she finds herself in today, and if she is to reverse her economic fortunes, she must first tackle this lack of productivity and move from net consumers to net producers of goods and services. This consumerist nature is not peculiar to black people on Continental Africa, even African Americans are known to be net consumers in the American business equation. Dr. Claud Anderson, President of The Harvard Institute, a US Black think tank that works to help African Americans become self-sufficient and economically competitive is credited with the saying, "Black people have enriched every group except themselves."

In the Bible, the Parable of the Talents in the book of Matthew 25: 14 – 30 is a perfect illustration of the economic disadvantage most of Africa and people of African descent appear to be saddled with. For readers, not familiar with the gospels I will summarize the parable. The story was told of a man setting off to a far country who decided to share resources called talents among his three servants. To one he gave five, to another two and to the third just one talent. After a long time, this man returned and called these three servants to *settle accounts* with them. The first traded with his five talents and had five more to present, the second similarly traded with his two and had two more to present, while the third servant did nothing with his talent. To make matters worse, the third servant went on and on about how their master was fond of reaping where he did not sow, which is where the story gets interesting. The talent was taken from the third servant and given to the guy who had ten, not even to the fellow who had four as the socialists within us all would expect. The next thing the investor says is what baffles many Christians. He says in verse 29 (NKJV), *"For to everyone who has, more will be given, and he will have abundance, but from him who does not have, even what he has will be taken away."* Wow! This reads like something off some business journal, yet these are the basic tenets of capitalism. The rich and those astute with wealth get richer, while the less entrepreneurial get poorer, and right now, this third servant is looking like the Motherland, while the other two servants are the developed world.

More Africans need to shed our consumerist laid back leanings and become more entrepreneurial, so that the few *talents* we have are no longer taken away from us. This requires a kind of social re-engineering that will cause a critical mass of Africans and people of color in general to individually develop a desire to break forth and succeed. The greatest obstacle to developing desire within people generally regardless of race is our conviction that we will never be able to satisfy the desire and so a self-defense mechanism within us tells us that the safest course of action is to avoid the desire and avoid the frustration. John Galbraith calls this process "accommodating to poverty" and points out that people always choose the economic level they will accept – it is never thrust on them. This is a bit like a guy crushing on a girl and dying in silence to avoid the heartache of a rejection, and in the end never gets the girl; but don't we all know that *fortune favors the bold?*

As is usual with behavioral matters of this nature, not just in developing countries but with the generality of people everywhere, there is a religious dimension to this problem of self-inflicted limitation. In Christendom for instance we have verses of scripture like Philippians 4:11 (NKJV), in which the apostle Paul says "*... for I have learned in whatever state I am, to be content*", which is misconstrued by some faithful as an excuse not to make any genuine effort to improve their lot. They mix up laziness with contentment, small time thinking with spirituality, and fear with humility. Hence my earlier call for social re-engineering or *re-orientation* that will cause a significant portion of the population to become dissatisfied with the status quo and determined to make a change.

In the first 15 years that ushered in the twenty first century sub-Saharan African economies expanded at an average rate of 5% a year, enough to have doubled Gross Domestic Product GDP output over the period. The continent was aided largely by commodities boom that was mostly due by rapid urbanization in China. As China's economy slowed, the prices of many commodities mined in Africa dropped. Copper for example, sold for about half as much as it did when it was at its peak. This in turn hit Africa's growth leading many to fret that the old pattern of commodity driven boom and bust in the continent was about to rear its ugly head again. The main underlying reason for this was that the manufacturing sectors of many African states missed out on the boom.

For economies like Nigeria who had squandered the proceeds from the 15 years' commodities boom, the reality of our excesses dawned on us when we went into a prolonged recession in 2016. Some two years earlier, I was in a discussion with a group of Indian businessmen about the economic trends in Nigeria when I shocked the group with my hope that the nation should run out of crude oil sooner than later for its own good. They were of course surprised by my statement, but my prayer was not out of bad will for my country. I was rather concerned that if this natural resource which should have been a blessing and an opportunity for rapid development, which we had turned into a curse did not cease to flow, our leaders would continue to waste its proceeds with impunity. In 2016, we had not run of oil, but the next *best* thing happened – oil prices were not what they were and if trends are anything to go by, prices would continue to slide for some time to come as technology improves on energy alternatives. The good news in Nigeria is that oil prices have caused a forced diversification of the economy. As at the time of writing this book in 2018, reports had it that oil accounted for just fifteen percent of her economy; a major leap from about fifty percent just decades earlier.

Name any country in Africa, and you could find world-class firms there at the turn of the twenty first century. Unfortunately, ten years later, you would go back and still find just the one firm. Whereas, in countries like Cambodia and Vietnam, you would go back and find 50 new firms. To be clear, it is not unheard of for countries to deindustrialise as they grow richer, because growth in service-based sectors of the economy such as entertainment, helps shrink manufacturing's slice of the total GDP. But many African countries are deindustrialising while still poor, raising the worrying prospect that they will miss out on the chance to grow rich by shifting workers from farms to higher-paying factory jobs. Premature deindustrialisation is not just happening in Africa—other developing countries are also seeing the growth of factories slowing, partly because technology is reducing the demand for low-skilled workers.

"Manufacturing has become less labour intensive across the board," says Margaret McMillan of Tufts University. That means that it is hard, and getting harder, for African firms to create jobs in the same numbers that Asian ones did from the 1970s onwards. Yet deindustrialisation appears to be hitting African countries hard. This is partly because weak infrastructure drives up the costs of production. The African Development Bank found in 2010 that electricity, costs three times more on average in Africa than it does in South Asia. Poor roads and congested ports also drive up the cost of transportation (Economist 2015).

Another disadvantage for the continent is, perversely, its bounty of natural riches. As mentioned earlier, booming commodity prices brings with it the "Dutch disease": economies benefiting from increased exports of oil and the like seeing their exchange rates driven up, which then makes it cheaper to import goods and services, and harder to produce and export locally manufactured goods.

Africa's final problem is its geography. East Asia's string of successes happened under the "flying geese" model of development, where a "lead" nation creates a slipstream for other nations in the region to follow. This happened first in the 1970s, when Japan moved labour-intensive manufacturing to Taiwan and South Korea. But Africa seems to have missed the flock. "We don't have a leading goose, a Japan," says Ngozi Okonjo-Iweala, Nigeria's former finance minister. Light manufacturing is being moved out of China to neighbouring Bangladesh and Vietnam and not distant Africa, despite its promise of plentiful cheap labour. "Africa's growth is not driven by export-led manufacturing," says Dani Rodrik, an economist. "And in the coming century Africa will find it difficult to grow through that route."

Yet some African states are bucking the trend. Ethiopia's manufacturing for instance, has grown by an average of 10% a year in the last decade, albeit from a very low base, partly because it has courted foreign investors. "We approached Holland's horticultural firms, China's textile and leather firms and Turkey's garment firms. Now we're bringing in German and Swiss pharmaceuticals," says Arkebe Oqubay, a minister who promotes Ethiopia's industrialisation. Ethiopia is not alone. Tanzania's manufacturing output has grown at an average of 7.5% annually in the last decade also. This it has done by wooing Chinese and Singaporean clothing firms and starting construction on its first mega port and industrial park in 2015.

Nonetheless, factories are not creating nearly enough jobs for the millions of young people moving into African cities each year. Most of them end up under-employed or in part-time employment in low-productivity businesses such as groceries or restaurants, which are limited by the tiny domestic economy. A report noted that Africa currently generates only two percent of the global demand for goods and services. To grow fast,

African countries need to shift workers into more productive industries. Their governments need to provide the infrastructure and the incentives for manufacturing firms to set up. Without determined action, we risk another lost decade as the commodity bust deepens.

Africa needs to reverse this trend by shedding her taste for foreign products and growing the two percent of world demand which, she generates. The first step to doing this is to identify areas of competitive advantage where we could compete and begin building capacity in those sectors. For starters, we can begin adding value to our commodities and exporting semi-processed or finished products. We need to grow and produce more of what we consume. We need to begin to imbibe the culture of patronizing made in Africa goods, and stop writing them off in preference to foreign goods and services. A valid example is the positive development in the Nigerian construction industry, in which locally made building materials are now preferred to imported ones. This trend needs to take root in all other sectors of African economies including, food, clothing, household goods, tourism, entertainment, automotive industry just to name a few.

In the energy sector, less and less hydrocarbons now leave the continent and instead are now being used in generating more electricity locally. Eco bank (a Pan African Bank) reported "Sub-Saharan gas production has been boosted significantly by rising demand for power following the completion of several gas-fired power plants in Nigeria, Ghana, Gabon and Cote d'Ivoire." This is a positive development for the continent and signals economic growth. Big gas projects in Equatorial Guinea, Mozambique and Tanzania largely targeted at export markets were ongoing as at the time of writing this book. This may not impress readers more interested in sustainability; however, this growth is also being felt with renewable energy on the continent. Falling costs with solar energy in particular is largely responsible for this, which is a no-brainer considering most of the continent's year-round summer conditions – a result of its asymmetric location right on the equator. The International Energy

Agency (IEA) estimates that Africa added nearly 4.5 GW of power to its grids from renewable sources in 2016 alone.

The African aviation sector is another area of concern. In the 1970s and 80s, African skies were awash with the likes of Air Afrique, Nigerian Airways, Ghana Airways, Air Tanzania, Kenya Airways, et cetera. However, by the 90s and early 2000, these airlines were comatose owing to corruption, government intervention and poor management. They were in huge debts and depended on government handouts to pay salaries and to maintain their fleets. They became, as it were, drains on government revenue and instead of promoting the brand of their countries they had become embarrassments to their governments.

These years also coincided with the great wave of privatization and commercialization, which blew away many airlines. Some like Kenya Airways were privatized and handed over to the private sector to run. Others like Air Afrique and Nigeria Airways were liquidated, while others like Air Mauritius continued to run at constant financial loss to their owners. For those that were liquidated, foreign operators have stepped in and capitalized on the absence of national carriers. In the case of Nigeria Airways, because of the absence of a national carrier to fly direct to the major cities of the world, flights out of Lagos, Abuja and Port Harcourt (the major international airports in the country) operated by foreign operators are packed to the rafters. This obtains even though business-class and upper-class cabins go for higher than a national carrier would charge. No African nation with a population of more than sixty million should be without a national carrier. Best practices at success stories like Ethiopian Airlines, South African Airlines and Egypt Air should be benchmarked by the rest of the continent to plug this major source of revenue loss to the continent. Africa has missed the third industrial revolution and cannot afford to miss a fourth Industrial revolution.

The United Nations' seventeen Sustainable Development Goals (SDGs) to transform the world by 2030 are meant to carry on the momentum generated by the eight Millennium Development Goals (MDGs) and fit into a global development framework beyond 2015 when the MDGs expired. The SDGs are an improvement on the MDGs in that they focus on building a sustainable world where environmental sustainability and social inclusion are equally valued alongside economic development.

The former Liberian President and first female president of any African country, Ellen Johnson Sirleaf once said, "The size of your dreams must always exceed your current capacity to achieve them, if your dreams do not scare you, then they are not big enough." Africa needs to prove the skeptics who doubt her wrong. Africa needs to dream big. In dreaming big and becoming more productive, she must also strive for excellence and perfection. It is not enough to do things just for the sake of doing them; the culture of excellence through continuous improvement must accompany productivity. This is necessary to become competitive in the global market place.

I recall from my years working for a multinational in Africa that project costs in my country are usually at least, twice or thrice the cost in developed countries despite limited resources. The reason for this is quite simple – literally everything is imported, even expatriate manpower to supervise the projects. Why? In my opinion, this is due to the lack of the spirit of excellence and continuous improvement with local talent. The good news however, is that even this trend is beginning to change as more and more multinationals are not only downsizing expatriate man-power across the continent and Asia, but are now sending Africans and people from developing countries on expat assignments to other parts of the world. These decisions used to be purely for cost optimization in the past, but now more of these postings are merit based as indigenous talent begin to match and exceed their peers around the world.

This culture of continuous improvement and being thorough in general ties in with the qualities I listed earlier in the chapter; ethics, integrity, love for work and being productive. There are two sides to this culture of continuous improvement; there is the supplier side and the customer side. The customer firstly must have zero tolerance to products or services that do not meet pre-agreed specifications with penalties for nonperformance. This forces the product or service provider to up his or her game to stay relevant in the business. When people continuously tolerate mediocre services or products and do not raise the bar for providers of such services and products, they are inadvertently saying that it is okay to be average or mediocre at *this*. In the public procurement space of the public sector, millions of dollars are continuously lost because of either misplaced tribal and sectarian sentiments as I mentioned earlier, or collusion between civil servants (meant to certify completion of public projects) and contractors, to the detriment of the public who are beneficiaries of such projects.

It is not possible to overstress or belabor this point on embracing a continuous improvement culture –that philosophy of getting a little bit better at something every single day – because this is a major opportunity area for Africa and the developing world. A more general term for this is a "Learning Culture". A learning culture is one that values the acquisition of knowledge and skills for application in the workplace and other facets of life. However, it is easier to teach a learning culture in an organization whether private or public. All that is required is for the management to buy into the idea, share the expectations with employees and do the enabling work such as trainings, goal setting, et cetera. However, when the informal sector is accountable for a sizeable portion of your economy's private sector, driving a learning culture becomes a bit more difficult.

In developing countries, most new jobs are being created in the so-called informal sector. The informal sector comprises Micro and Small Enterprises (MSEs) with workforce between one and upwards of ten to fifteen people. These businesses are usually short term focused with commission-based remuneration. Skill sets of the group will most times be determined by the owner's mastery. Most of these business owners are not strategic enough in their thinking to invest in trainings or new and improved ways of doing things – unless there is a threat from competition that puts him at risk of becoming less competitive and being forced out of business. It is either that, or the local market embraces some game changing technology or a new benchmark best practice that causes a step change in the area of specialty. Yet this is the sector that provides most of the trades and semi-skilled labor in these societies. In this kind of business environment, a learning culture can only be embraced by the business when paying customers consistently insist on better quality products and services or just better value for their money. A feedback mechanism is anyways the main driver for any self-correcting, self-improving system.

Unfortunately, despite the good intentions of any *demanding* customers (this includes superiors and colleagues in the workplace), in the African society, there is always an extent beyond which it becomes difficult to insist on better performance. Why? For some strange reason, black people easily get sentimental and begin to personalize what essentially should be business decisions. In fact, in my experience I believe it is easier for a foreigner to make more demands on Africans than for Africans to do so of themselves. The recipient of the feedback would usually rather than objectively focusing on the benefits of the performance issues raised, instead opt to whip up needless sentiment with his compatriot or fellow black man. God forbid these two parties belong to different tribes or practice different faiths – in which case what should have been a push for excellence can easily blow up into full scale tribal or sectarian confrontation, that may not stop with just the parties involved, but sometimes fellow tribesmen and faithful get dragged into the melee. Africans and people of African descent must learn to get along and stop allowing minor misunderstandings to create chasms and stall progress in our communities. This is one of the many challenges confronting productivity improvement in Africa and the developing world. Some governments are adopting policies that supply a pipeline of training services for workers in the informal sector, as a way of instilling a much-desired learning culture in the society.

These are rudimentary issues developed countries no longer (if they ever) have to contend with. In the summer of 2016, I was opportune to visit one of the numerous Toyota (originally Toyoda) assembly plants in Toyota, Aichi, Japan and see firsthand the origins of world-famous Kanban and Kaizen systems. Anyone with a background in manufacturing can relate with the exhilaration of visiting the home of these and many other Japanese gifts to Industry. The Japanese not unlike other high-tech economies like

Germany could not have become the world power houses that they are without a deep-rooted self-improvement culture in literary every facet of their everyday life. The desire to seek perfection is drilled into the subconscious of their workforce through their school system as well as general societal expectation to the point that; it has almost become a crime to produce anything average or mediocre. When I juxtapose this next to the quality of jobs my brothers and sisters are comfortable with in my homeland and other developing countries – whether it be simple things like uneven stairs or missing bolts and screws from a car fresh out of a garage – you realize why continuous improvement is needed to first secure local patronage in the continent before even looking for outside patronage.

The same reasoning you could say plays out in governance – complacency by people who do not insist on good governance results in mediocre leadership due to lack of accountability by corrupt politicians and public officials in government. This is at the root of most underperforming sectors in Africa, even the agricultural sector or agribusiness. Africa with its thirty million square kilometers of land should not still be plagued by famines every time there is a drought. Agriculture should not only be guaranteeing food sufficiency but should also be a major foreign exchange earner for parts of the African continent.

When most people think of agriculture in Africa, images of poor and overworked farmers with crude tools on a rural farm readily come to mind. Many, especially young Africans, still think that agribusiness is a poor man's occupation. Nowadays everybody wants a white-collar office job in the city. Agribusiness is hardly on anyone's mind (Iwuoha 2017). We will discuss opportunities in agribusiness in a later chapter.

Of course, the problem of desert encroachment is becoming a challenge in the nations that surround the Sahara, but ground-breaking irrigation technology developed by the likes of Israel and more recently China are being used to recover deserts in Israel and neighboring states in the Arabic Peninsula. Africa can easily tap into these innovations to reverse desert encroachment problems on the continent.

So as not to be seen as belaboring the socioeconomic challenges in one continent and ignoring those of the rest of the developing world, Latin America, Central America and the Caribbean in particular are faced with similar challenges as Africa, though mostly in better shape relatively speaking.

By 2015, Latin America and the Caribbean had met most of the MDGs, a historical feat, especially with regard to poverty reduction, access to safe drinking water and primary education. From 2002 to 2013, close to 72 million people left poverty and some 94 million rose to the middle class. Even so, inequality continues to be a characteristic of the region. Latin America and the Caribbean are home to 10 of the world's 15 most unequal countries. According to our Human Development Report for the region, 38 percent, almost two in every five Latin Americans, are economically vulnerable today (Faieta 2017).

One of the things Latin America and the Caribbean have going for them is regional integration, though it can only play a limited role in the region because of the similarity of endowments between its countries. Intra-regional trade has remained at a persistent twenty percent, which is much less than the sixty percent in Europe and forty to fifty percent in East Asia, but still better than the sixteen percent in Africa.

The emergence of the Pacific Alliance, an ambitious and forward-looking integration scheme between Colombia, Chile, Mexico and Peru has revived a push for regional integration aimed at liberalizing the movement of goods, services, people and capital among participating countries. It is also a good platform to further strengthen trade relations with Asia-Pacific countries. Recent interest by Argentina in the Pacific Alliance, changing economic dynamics in the Southern Cone and a fresh interest in closer ties between Mexico, Brazil and Argentina, will surely bring a renewed momentum for integration in the region (Gonzalez 2017).

Deeper regional cooperation should take advantage of the proximity of nations and complimentary production of goods and services. It is a fact of life that economic activity is geographically clustered, be it due to lower trade costs or other factors of economic performance, like endowments and institutions, which are similar among neighboring countries. Policy-makers internationally recognize regional integration as vital to economic growth and trade, and therefore crucial for the creation of more and better jobs.

Despite efforts at regional integration the overwhelming sense is that the Americas at present are experiencing a geopolitical lull – free from major battles for regional influence, perhaps, but also devoid of any vision grand enough to unite all or significant part of the Americas. Unsurprisingly, China has increased its hemispheric influence, and has thus far used its sway to advance primarily economic aims rather than political ones.

China is no stranger to Latin America. Its trade with the region has multiplied 22 times since 2000, and governments in Latin America received over \$21 billion in financing from Chinese banks in 2016 alone. China's growing footprint in the region has been driven by economic interests, but diplomats have nonetheless observed shifting postures from Latin America on issues important to Beijing, such as territorial disputes in the Pacific. As President Xi Jinping works to seize the mantle of global statesmanship and Latin America adjusts to an absentee Uncle Sam, China may see an opportunity to step up its pursuit of political and diplomatic influence in the region (Camilleri et al 2018).

As I round up this chapter, I will like to quickly recap the points that are worthy of note. First and foremost, I mentioned that, clergy in developing countries would do their nations well by looking at the negative effects of overlaboring the prosperity gospel in their pulpits. Its psychological effect on individual motivation can be counter-productive to society, as it misleads people into thinking that a special relationship with God guarantees them prosperity even without any genuine effort on their part. Because religion plays a major role in these societies, the side effects of this doctrine cannot be ignored. Alongside there should be a restructuring of educational systems to include more hands-on training with a more practical oriented curriculum and less of theoretical studies; there is no point having a *complete* curriculum if the workshops that should enable students translate theory into practice is missing. This may require increased educational funding and more partnership between higher institutions and industry. However, in the long run it will give fresh school leavers head starts in life by making them better prepared for life as they leave school. People from developing economies must learn to put aside sectarian and ethnic differences in the workplace, to embrace a learning culture of continuous improvement, as it is indispensable in any society serious about increasing productivity. Without this positive attitude, one can easily lose pace and eventually fall behind an already very competitive, dynamic and ever-changing, fast-paced world. In addition, agribusiness is a sector where quick and easy victories can be won considering the continent is traditionally agrarian. All that is required is the quick adoption of modern mechanized farming and animal husbandry techniques to increase yield and replace the archaic manual methods of generations past.

Finally, there is the challenge of getting the macro and micro economics right. This depends heavily in the ability of leadership to draft the best technocrats into government who can guide the politicians in the arduous task of policy formulation and implementation. It sounds so simple, but sectarianism, tribalism and nepotism continue to keep competent hands out of government, leaving us with the problem of square pegs in round government holes. The private sector is not immune to these same problems. The main difference is more focus on results in the private sector as non-performance is less likely to be tolerated for a long time by business owners keen on returns on their investment.

With these foundational issues tackled, Africa and other developing countries can focus on the task of increased productivity, continuously improving output and growing Gross Domestic Product (GDP). Increased productivity will lead to more favorable trade balances, and eventually prosperous trade as opposed to aid from the developed world. All these bearing in mind that the developed world is not sitting on its laurels waiting for the less developed to catch up; true to the culture of excellence and continuous improvement, they are working on the next big thing such as, sustainable energy and artificial intelligence. Hence the challenge before Africa and other developing countries as they focus on the task of increased productivity is that such concerted efforts must bring about *rapid* development. Anything short of rapid development will not be adequate and could be deemed as failure. All hands must be put to the plough and excuses like neo-colonial structures and endemic corruption will have to be swept aside as soon as is humanly possible, so that we can face the humungous task at hand.

CHAPTER 4

LEADERSHIP 101

I n my research for this book I came upon several definitions of Leadership, but the one I liked most is "the ability to inspire and organize people towards actualizing a pre-conceived set of goals "(Adeyemi 2017). An excellent example is a conductor leading an orchestra to the pre-conceived goal of delivering a beautiful symphony. These set of goals could be positive or negative, either way it does not make the orchestrator (conductor) any less of a leader. But societal norms dictate that leadership goals should be positive, and that is why the likes of Adolf Hitler though a great leader in almost every sense of the word is still loathed till this day - at least by most people. John Maxwell, a renowned expert on the subject defined leadership simply as *Influence*. Goals are conceived as a vision, and the leader uses influence to orchestrate resources including people, capital, et cetera, to deliver a preconceived set of goals.

During pre-independence in Africa, a fearless generation of leaders fought tooth and nail for the liberation of the continent. They had visions of what their nations should be like once the right to self-determination was returned to the rightful owners of the land. This led to their fight to successfully lead their nations to independence from colonial rule, and that essentially was where Africa's problems took a different dimension. African leaders at independence did not know how to handle the combustible mix of the foreign colonial institutions they inherited and the complex societies comprising tribes with differing idiosyncrasies. This included countrymen from other tribes, when just decades before they only had fellow tribesmen to contend with. Thus, the task was to fashion out ways not just to co-exist but to thrive using the strange new institutions left by the colonials, a daunting task you must agree. They had to take complex social systems i.e. capitalism, democracy or even communism from one part of the world, and ship it to Africa for implementation, like a plug and play module and a missing part of some bigger machine.

Experience around the world has proven that this does not always work. Nations have spent decades experimenting with different forms of social systems and some are still struggling to get it right to this day. People need to learn from errors and evolve their own social system and choose how they want to be governed without interference from external parties. Along with the rest of the developing world, Africa is having to hasten its journey of evolving its own institutions and brand of democracy. These institutions will have to cope with the uniqueness and diverseness of cultures in our countries.

Today, political institutions in some African countries are saddled with self-serving politicians who have little interest in serving people who vote them into office. A good number aspire for office not driven by any people centered vision, but they only want the recognition and perks that go with the position, not to mention an opportunity to loot the treasury. This is made possible because of weak institutions, weak law enforcement agencies and limited jurisprudence. I will again use my home country as an example. Most strong democracies have evolved into two party political systems where elections are mainly contests between two major parties who have at their core differing political ideology; while other parties are platforms for other interest groups and movements to air their political views at the legislative arm of government.

In my country, parties are not known for any particular political ideology. The party manifesto is malleable and can swing from one political ideology to the other overnight, depending on what the politicians think is pressing to the people in the build up to the next election. Unfortunately, party primaries and voting at the elections continue to be mainly along ethnic and religious lines. This often can be linked to the fact that these nations are sometimes unions of strange bedfellows in that they are a collection of different people who historically may even have been hostile neighbors but found themselves foisted together by colonial fiat. Therefore, loyalty to the tribe or sect most times unfortunately supersedes loyalty to the nation. This affects patriotism by inadvertently playing out as tribalism or sectarianism. In Kenya for instance, the rivalry in the last few elections have been between the Kikuyu and Luo tribes, two tribes whom from my research, probably hardly ever had major interactions before 1901.

Here's a story that happened in my country between 1983 and 1985. A certain Peter Onu (an Igbo Christian) of Nigeria was Acting Secretary-General of the then Organization of African Unity (OAU), now African Union (AU). At the 1985 summit in Addis Ababa, statesmen like Julius Nyerere, President of Tanzania, lobbied for his election as substantive Secretary-General. However, there was a major stumbling block to Peter Onu's candidature: his military Head of State, Major General Muhammadu Buhari (a Fulani Muslim) was campaigning against him. Buhari, in his national broadcast had earlier said: "This generation of Nigerians and indeed future generations have no other country than Nigeria." But when the crunch came, his allegiance to Nigeria disappeared. In the election of the OAU Secretary-General in 1985, Buhari voted against Nigeria and for Niger (Nigeria's neighbor to the north) instead. He secured the election of Ide Oumarou, a Fulani man from Niger, as opposed to his compatriot, an Igbo man from Nigeria. By so doing, Buhari became the first Head of State in the history of the African Union and possibly modern international relations to vote against his country in favor of his tribe. Little surprise then that his second coming as a civilian President in 2015 was ridden with accusations of nepotism and sectionalism in appointments into his government.

A good antidote to this kind of thinking is a quote from the dad of an old college acquaintance of mine who was President of the Nigerian Senate in 2000, the late Dr. Chuba Okadigbo. He is quoted as having said," If you are emotionally attached to your tribe, religion or political leaning to the point that truth and justice become secondary considerations, your education is useless, your exposure is useless." And to that list of emotional attachments I add "your race".

But I digress; my point here is that some African nations in their composition have already been dealt a poor hand, as their ethnic and religious identities within the national identity cloud the judgement of the average citizen. In multiethnic African countries, there is usually an overwhelming effort at balancing equal representation from federating ethnicities and merit in national institutions. Due to the varying education levels in different parts of the country; basing admissions and appointments purely on merit will sideline educationally disadvantaged parts of the country. The flip side of this is that in ensuring national spread merit is thrown out of the window, such that in the end you may find more square pegs in round holes. This balancing act plays out at literally all levels of society. For example, admissions into colleges and higher institutions, recruitment of staff into government jobs and appointments into boards of national companies and government positions.

In my country for instance, there is an unconstitutional gentlemen's agreement in the major political parties on rotation of the presidency between the mostly Muslim North and the mostly Christian South. To court votes from the other region, such a candidate always must have a vice president from the other region such that if any major issues come up during the tenure of a president that might warrant parliamentary action such as an impeachment, the president's region always views it as an attempt to usurp them of their turn at governance. In the end, the entire nation suffers and must endure till the end of the tenure before any hope of change can be made to an underperforming government. The result, mediocrity holds sway over meritocracy.

African nations need to find a way to make elections less about ethnic and sectarian differences and more about policy thrust and ideology of candidates seeking political office. The good news is, this is already happening. During the very election that President Buhari was elected into office in 2015, Christians and people of different ethnicities living in the South West and North Central regions of the country voted massively for this Muslim even though he had a history of backing some hardline Islamic views. They voted him nonetheless because they were fed up of corruption that the then incumbent Christian from the South – Goodluck Jonathan – had tolerated during his administration. This made Buhari's victory one based on outstanding issues as opposed to ethnic sentiments for a change.

This kind of voting outside ethnic and religious lines was possible because of the literacy levels in the southern part of the country. Voting outside ethnic and religious lines would be difficult in the north if not outright impossible due to low literacy levels in that part of the country. In populations with a preponderance of uneducated people, it is difficult to get people to shed ethnic and religious considerations in elections and other topical issues. This is the reason why it is *strategic* for the Northern elite to stall educational development in their regions, so that they can split people along ethnic and religious lines when it serves them, such as during elections. These kinds of leaders represent an old order of African leadership that is gradually being phased out and replaced by new young dynamic leaders who do not foster and exaggerate ethnic differences for political gain but focus on fixing issues that are important to the people.

Ordinarily tribalism does not necessarily have to weaken patriotism. Love for people of common heritage is nothing new in any part of the world. In any crowd, it is normal to look out for people with whom one shares things in common. There is always the reassurance that at least, "I can be at ease with this fellow as he or she should understand my idiosyncrasies and appreciate my humor." It is a knowledge of shared history and culture that binds a people together in tribalism and there is nothing superficially wrong with that. The problem only sets in where a bias for tribe begins to affect the shared common interest of other member tribes or compatriots with a different creed. This is pronounced in Africa where the sense of shared history is more with tribesmen than with fellow compatriots. Albeit, the new nation states in Africa have only been in existence for roughly little more than a century. In addition, I recall a certain Pope once said to a certain American President "… after all, what is two hundred years in the life of a nation?" I am convinced that as time goes by and histories are written; un-inhibited cross settlement between tribes, inter-tribal marriages, religious tolerance and social cohesion continue; it is only a matter of time before nationalism and patriotism begins to trump tribal and religious considerations in everyday life until one's nation becomes one's tribe among Africans.

Another unfortunate development in our political space worth mentioning is the way some politicians switch party affiliation before and after elections. In the run-up to elections, political heavy weights begin carpet crossing between parties like escorts switching allegiance for the *right price*. Then after the elections, another round of carpet crossing takes place. This time politicians decamp in droves to the winning party with the hope of taking part in the sharing of *spoils* in appointments, contracts, committee memberships and sale of government assets overseen by the Executive at both federal and state government levels. This perennial switching of allegiance is possible because like I mentioned earlier, the political parties do not have any particular political ideology. Of course, you cannot expect politicians produced by such a system to have enough character to be capable of maintaining their positions on issues they previously had strong convictions about. Some of these carpet crossers win elections on other party platforms only to *port* to the party that clinches the presidency during their tenures. It is a bit like Bernie Sanders switching to the Republican party shortly after the Democrats lost the 2016 elections – ridiculous, isn't it? Some of our politicians have switched in and out of one political party more than twice in their political careers. Imagine voting out a certain crop of politicians in an election, only to find they have moved to the party you voted in few months down the line. The electorate find themselves stuck in a rot, where regardless what they do at the next election, they are stuck with the same set of crooked politicians. It is one of those, *you're damned if you do and you are damned if you don't* situations. How can anyone expect these *musical chair type politicians* to possibly have anything of lasting value to offer the electorate?

However, it could be worse. I have friends from North Africa who tell me that we should consider ourselves lucky to even have a semblance of an opposition in our country, because in some of their countries every form of opposition is stifled at infancy. I was in Cairo in the spring of 2018 and whilst they were two weeks in the lead up to a presidential election, there were no signs on the streets or in the media that anyone else was vying for office with the incumbent. This is despite a revolution in that country seven years earlier that dethroned the then sit tight President Hosni Mubarak. In the "Democratic" Republic of Congo, presidential elections have been postponed since 2016. The latest date for elections (fingers crossed) now December 2018, though in the case of the DRC, at the time of writing this book, the incumbent shows no sign of contesting. It is evident that a Western style democracy may not be replicable everywhere in the world.

Democracy should be about the will of a majority prevailing instead of an elite few. In an effort to be democratic, it is easy to get caught up in putting every major decision to a vote or a referendum. However, in the end the major task that leaders are saddled with is decision making. We all have varying heuristic tendencies which cause us to react differently to the same set of information and hence decide differently. Anyone that is part of any larger organization knows that strategic information comes from the top and trickles down the hierarchy on a need to know basis. So, in the end leaders will always be privy to information not accessible to the people they lead. Every democracy must decide for itself that point where elected leaders can be allowed to make the best judgement on behalf of the electorate. But what must be common to all these democracies is a transparent electoral process that guarantees that only the people's choice emerges at the end of the process. Aside from that, every nation needs to evolve its own form of democracy that works for its unique set of circumstances and strengthen democratic institutions as it does so.

The thirty-fifth president of the United States, J F Kennedy in 1960 said, "A society whose young men and women are in a constant state of slumber will never realize her potentials". African youth must take responsibility. Africans must unite and vehemently fight corrupt leaders who run down our countries, cause their supporters to lose their lives during elections and mismanage their economies. Some Heads of State run to the International Monetary Fund (IMF) as though the IMF is "Santa Claus", rocking up international debts for unborn generations and further enslaving the continent. Nowhere is Texas Guinan's (American actress who died before World War II) quote truer than in Africa, "A politician is a fellow who will lay down *your* life for his country".

It is said that a people get the kind of leadership they *deserve*, which is another way of saying, people get the kind of leadership they *allow*. I agree with this. The late Howard Zinn an American historian, playwright, social activist and a political science professor at Boston University said and I quote, "Civil disobedience is not our problem. Our problem is civil obedience. Our problem is that people all over the world have obeyed the dictates of leaders... and millions have been killed because of this obedience... Our problem is that people are obedient all over the world in the face of poverty and starvation and stupidity, and war, and cruelty. Our problem is that people are obedient while the jails are full of petty thieves... (and) the grand thieves are running the country, That's our problem." Zinn, I read considered himself an anarchist but, in my opinion, his kind of thinking is needed now more than ever in developing nations. He would have been in impressed by the Arab spring which started just after his death in 2010.

I honestly do not know how African leaders can live with images of young Africans who regardless of all the risks transverse the Sahara and use rickety over crowded boats across the Mediterranean to get into Europe. It is the failure of their home states to provide them with opportunities that force them in desperation to embark on these perilous journeys. This happens despite the eighteenth-century-style human rights violations they suffer in route at the hands of fellow Africans. The latest dimension to Europe's refugee crisis is street markets in Libya, where sub-Saharan African migrants are sold as slaves. The fallout of Europe's "deal" with North African states to *hold on to illegal migrants and not let them cross their borders, in exchange for a few million euros.* These illegal migrants flee their homes in both the Middle-East and Africa; their pictures and stories doing more to perpetuate racism than traditions of acquired racial bias handed down from generation to generation. The racists justifying their bias by arguing that "if these third world nations cannot do something as simple as fixing their nations, then they are not deserving of their respect." The failure of Middle Eastern and African leadership to create institutions and policies that will put their regions on course to recovery continues to drive these young people to settle for being refugees and even slaves in other countries, rather than face hopelessness in their home states.

In his address at the 2014 Africa Development Bank Annual Meeting which he hosted, the Rwandan President Paul Kagame criticized bad African leaders for not doing enough to resolve crisis and problems affecting their people. Instead of these leaders traveling to places like France for photo opportunities with the world media to discuss the very same problems they could resolve within themselves or at worst within the continent. He said this practice made no sense and did not speak well of leadership on the continent.

An immigration crisis similar to that in the Mediterranean has developed in the United States' southern border with Mexico in the last couple of decades. While migrants may have been making the land border crossing into the United States for much of the last century, most of this illegal immigration was tolerated due to labor shortfalls in the USA at that time. Migrants are still fleeing the same economic conditions that drove their forerunners across the border decades earlier, with the added dimension of insecurity resulting from gang related violence by drug cartels in their home countries. The reasons for this are not farfetched as the socio-economic situation in Central America and the Caribbean is not too dis-similar from what obtains in Africa and at times worse as is the case with violent crimes.

The Northern Triangle of Central America — Guatemala, Honduras, and El Salvador — are the most violent countries in the world outside of formal combat zones. This is not a crisis that developed overnight. It is something that actually peaked in the '90s, when El Salvador was the most violent country in the world, with a homicide rate of 100 per 100,000. As at 2014, Honduras was on top with a figure around 90 or 91 per 100,000. In some countries, including Guatemala, the homicides rates have started a modest decline, but you cannot only look at homicide rates to gauge the levels of violence in society (Matthews 2014).

For instance, there was a gang truce in El Salvador that reduced homicide rates significantly, but extortion of small business owners, people in the informal economy, in open markets, and commuters, et cetera, has either continued or actually increased, and that is a huge problem. People continue to be kidnapped for ransom and assaulted. Thus, the problem of violence needs to be understood in terms of the numerous threats to citizens' security that include but are not limited to murders.

Therefore, as is the case with the migration crisis in the Mediterranean, not much can be done about the southern US migration crisis without political will and political leadership in Central America. Something drastic needs to be done to tackle the socioeconomic conditions that allow the cartels and gangs who perpetrate violence to flourish, if there is to be any hope of discouraging illegal migration. So many parallels can be drawn between Central America and the Caribbean on the one hand, and Africa and the Middle East on the other hand. For instance, with the exception of countries like Mexico (who was the colonizing power in the region), Costa Rica, El Salvador, Guatemala, Honduras and Nicaragua in Central America and the Dominican Republic and Haiti in the Caribbean, much of the remaining nations in these regions similar to Africa and the Middle East, gained independence from their colonials in the twentieth century and are therefore, still struggling with many of the economic issues highlighted for Africa earlier. The political terrain is unsurprisingly similar also, as Latin America has traditionally been home to dictators; charismatic men who had almost complete control over their nations for years, sometimes even decades. Some have been benign, some cruel and ruthless, and others somewhat peculiar, same as in the Middle East and Africa in the last century. The result is that while the rest of the world were developing and moving forward, these regions were hamstrung and stagnated by authoritarian regimes and now must play catch up.

In the last chapter, I wrote on the need for social re-engineering to raise a significant number of entrepreneurs. Again, it is not enough for just a few leaders in a country to have the right leadership mindset. A critical mass of new leadership – servant leaders – need to be voted into to power before any realistic change can be achieved. In the current state of performing below par, the less competent politicians in their midst will otherwise always carry the day. This new leadership would have the enormous task of establishing and strengthening institutions in these developing countries. In addition, this new crop of leaders would need to be allowed time by the populace to correct the ills of the past and ensure continuance of their policies. Succession planning would be needed to ensure any gains are sustained. The corruption and maladministration that set Africa back for instance, has eaten too deep and will take decades to reverse.

It has not been all bad news around the continent as a few nations have made some progress down this path. In West Africa, Ghana for instance continues to strengthen its democratic institutions after the revolution led by Jerry Rowlings in 1979. In East Africa, Tanzania from the time of President Julius Nyerere to more recently President John Magufuli has continued to sustain relatively high economic growth averaging 6 – 7% a year, as well as strengthen democratic institutions. Magufuli may be the first on the continent to seriously tackle tax evasion by multinational corporations with what foreign investors menacingly call "resource nationalism". Hopefully other African nations will catch on to this. In the South, a great political precedence was set in South Africa on February

14th, 2018, when the ruling African National Congress (ANC) forced President Jacob Zuma to resign following years of alleged corruption among other allegations unbecoming of a commander in chief. These great strides need to be sustained and replicated across the continent. The strengthening of democratic institutions is the foundation of any real progress in the developing world.

A very good example of a developing nation which has successfully strengthened its democratic institutions since independence from the British colonials in 1947, and incidentally doubles as the largest democracy in the world is India. Their success story can be linked to many positive developments in the political space in India. The fact that opposition parties have been allowed consistently over the years to keep ruling parties in check, plus their ability to repeatedly conduct transparent elections for more than 700 million voters (a feat in itself), has helped inculcate a spirit of accountability in their ruling class. This character in leadership is indispensable for any nation serious about strengthening its democratic institutions. The Prime Minister at the time of putting this book together, Shri Narendra Modi, exemplifies the character of accountability and servant leadership sought in leading any nation.

Shri Narendra Modi's effort into politics has been a constant effort and not an overnight turn up. His vision and actions were not just systematic but also organized. With no strong political family background, he managed to lead one of the world's largest democracies. He has been working hard on his dreams of making India a successful economy. Right from his foresightedness for demonetization, to making Adhaar card mandatory and his Swachh Bharat Initiative of making India clean (Kumari 2018).

Modi's tough (and sometimes unpopular) economic reforms have not just put India on track to becoming the world's fastest-growing major economy in 2018, but also made him one of the most popular Indian leaders since Mahatma Gandhi (India's charismatic pre-independence leader who led India to independence and inspired movements for civil rights and freedom across the world).

Of course, it did not all happen overnight for India. Krishna Menon in *Democracy and Development in India* wrote, "In the years following independence, when the nationalist glow was still warm and reassuring, there was a kind of consensus built around the charismatic leadership of Jawaharlal Nehru. It was believed that India's economic problems were a result of colonialism, and with independence, the nationalist state would address and tackle this problem... By the end of the 1960s however the first cracks in this consensus began to emerge. This breakdown of consensus then sped along, and by the 1980s through many other tumultuous events of Indian politics, the challenge to the Nehruvian consensus became stronger, louder, and deeper... People's restlessness began to express itself in the form of numerous social movements that questioned the legitimacy of the Indian state and its policies. These movements repeatedly drew attention to the sharp inequalities and discriminations that continue to be a part of the Indian landscape." It is this kind of restlessness and realization by the people in any nation, of their role in forging a democratic society that is essential for entrenching and establishing the democratic culture and institutions foundational for economic development anywhere in the world.

It is important to take away from the Indian example the role the citizenry played in their democratic and economic developmental journey map, which reaffirms the fact that it takes more than just political leadership to move a nation forward. A vibrant and restless populace able to evoke the very important office of the citizen is equally, if not more important, than the politicians in a democracy. It takes leadership in all spheres of life, starting from the family – the basic unit of any society, through to the organized civil society willing to use civil disobedience to call government to order, if the circumstances warrant it. It is not enough to only resort to both conventional and social media to air views about unacceptable conduct of the ruling class, as has become common practice in many developing countries, especially my native country Nigeria. Here, social media platforms get phenomenal patronage with predominantly social debates and very little tangible effort taken towards forcing the government to act when needed. Civil marches, demonstrations and other forms of civil disobedience are literally non-existent in view of enormous social challenges in my homeland.

Let us come down to the most foundational leadership which is leadership in the basic unit of society, the family. Parents – fathers in particular – have the rudimentary responsibility of providing sound leadership in the family. Not just any kind of leadership but the servant type of leadership – a selfless leadership. This is not the time for absentee father stats to be on the rise as it is among African Americans. Africans need more servant leaders in every sphere of life. It is unfortunate that even among religious leaders in the continent, servant type leadership which Jesus Christ and the prophet Mohammed taught is lacking. How much more in the secular?

Another of the shortfalls I have observed with leadership in the African continent is a disproportionate focus on short-term needs while paying less attention to long-term legacy projects. We seem to concern ourselves with mostly immediate needs, those of our families and our communities. As soon as those needs are met, little consideration is given to future needs. It is almost like the majority thinking is "today has enough troubles of its own, tomorrow will take care of itself." On the individual level, you see this in the urge of low- and medium-income earners to wear *expensive* designer labels and drive *expensive* cars, when the reality is that most of these folks are a pay-check away from being broke.

I remember a conversation I had once with a colleague visiting from Europe in 2011; she quipped that the ladies in our office wore more designer labels than they did in her office in Europe. You would expect the opposite to be the case, given the differential in per capita income coupled with the fact that these labels are mostly European. But this line of reasoning means nothing to these my compatriots who are bent on communicating opulence, even if they do so on credit. This is not to say in any way, that only women have this need to show off *wealth*, as men on the continent are guiltier. Now I know people are free to spend their incomes as they like and indulge themselves as they see fit, but more Africans need to develop personal leadership and learn to delay gratification.

There is a difference between an income and a windfall, an income accrues weekly or monthly while a windfall is not certain and may come in six months, a year or even never. People make the mistake of maintaining lifestyles based on windfalls instead of income, and that is why you see a guy riding a bike today, tomorrow he is in a gas guzzling SUV and the same time next year he owns neither. This is due to lack of planning and the inability to delay self-gratification. It is not like we are not at all investment minded, it is just that considering the poverty levels on the continent, living expansive lifestyles before creating a sizeable asset base that will benefit not just oneself but those around is simply unwise. There are not enough safety nets in our societies. Middle class and working-class income families can so easily fall below the poverty line with the loss of a job or a business in Africa more than most other places in the world. This is due to a lack of social security, and the non-existence of a welfare state. This singular fact is the greatest barrier to rolling back corruption on the continent.

The same thinking plays out when politicians need to make choices on infrastructure for the electorate. Government officials saddled with the responsibility of building road infrastructure for instance, when they have to make a choice between a tarmac that will last ten years and one that will last thirty years for twice the cost, will typically jump at the cheaper option even when the funds are available for the longer lasting option. Usually their line of reasoning will go something like, "my tenure ends in four at most eight years, so let the next administration worry about the next twenty years" or "the more expensive options leaves the administration with less funds for other short-term, political point scoring projects." When the cumulative costs are added, they turn out to be *"penny wise, pound foolish"* decisions. In the end, the people must make do with poor infrastructure and the resultant effects on their businesses and livelihoods. The concept of having a master plan or making provision for idle capacity and allowing future generations to build upon the accomplishments of their forebears is quite foreign to Africa.

In a nutshell, a major *ingredient* missing with African leadership is a sense of doing things for posterity. Making the most of the present and caring less for what follows. Also, this is not just an issue with the politicians, but is a problem that goes all the way down to leadership in many African families. Some fathers are less concerned about the legacy they bequeath their children. I am constrained as a lay person in the social sciences to put a finger on the root cause of this problem, but my best guess is that it may be linked to a culture of deferred or delayed succession in African society which plays out in the political space. Africa like most other parts of the world is fundamentally patriarchal. But unlike the developed world where old men may struggle to remain relevant in the political space, it is young men and women who struggle for recognition in African politics.

Our cultures bestow on aged men the status of near oracles, based on the belief that they are custodians of wisdom. This belief at times makes septuagenarians and octogenarians appear infallible in some African societies. This is one of the reasons it is not uncommon to find a disproportionate number of political positions still occupied by elderly men, instead of retiring for younger politicians and influencing matters from behind the scenes. We have a popular saying that *"With age comes wisdom,"* but as Oscar Wilde put it, *"… but sometimes age comes alone."* A people cannot be caught up using twentieth century methods to tackle twenty first century problems, it just will not work. In Africa, we are more inclined to keep old politicians in power at the expense of vibrant newcomers. As you would expect, this almost guarantees stagnation in these countries and dwelling in the past instead of empowering and enabling the next generation in good time. The good news is that this does not obtain in the business space as the official retirement age ensures timely succession in both the public service and the corporate world, without which these sit-tight patriarchs would remain in service until they kick the bucket.

The end of Robert Mugabe's era as Zimbabwean president in November 2017 must serve as *a shot across the bow* for other sit tight African leaders like Teodoro Obiang in Equatorial Guinea, Yoweri Museveni in Uganda, Paul Biya in Cameroon and Omar al-Bashir in Sudan. Africa is gradually waking up to the reality that these old men and their ilk do not necessarily have the answers to their nation's problems. The forty-fourth and first African American President of the United States, Barack Obama put it perfectly when he said, "Africa doesn't need strong men, it needs strong institutions."

Stronger African institutions would for instance do a better job of protecting the continent from soaring debt burdens. As at 2016, only five sub-Saharan Africa nations, the DR Congo, Kenya, Nigeria, South Sudan and Botswana had total public debt less than thirty five percent of Gross Domestic Product. Very worrying among these debt profiles is the portion that comes in the name of aid which is really aid *mixed* with *concessional loans*. The Chinese are well known on the continent for giving this kind of "aid". These Aid are structured as Development Finance which is very different from Development Assistance as defined by the Organization for Economic Cooperation and Development (OECD), which China unsurprisingly is not a member of. It is estimated that by 2025, China would have provided Africa with one trillion dollars in financing including direct investment, soft loans and commercial loans. These concessional loans are usually targeted at infrastructure, which by itself is a good thing which creates needed employment.

However, because Development Financing is most times referred to as aid, the recipient countries sometimes overlook probing the executional details of the projects these funds finance. For instance, the Chinese companies that are awarded these projects sometimes do not comply with expatriate quotas in place in these African countries. In the end, African infrastructure is being built with Chinese loans that must be paid back with interest, by Chinese firms using disproportionate Chinese expatriate labor and less of local workforce. This is evident when driving past these construction sites, some foreign workers can be seen doing simpler tasks that do not require expat labor. Ordinarily this would not be an issue in countries where affordable manpower is lacking, but in Africa where youth unemployment can reach as high as twenty and thirty percent, this is simply incomprehensible. These lopsided agreements are the kinds of deals that are made in nations where nepotism is crippling the government, in that public officials are not chosen on merit but based on whom they know, and mediocrity continues to hold sway.

These projects are most times packaged as "technical assistance." An essential part of technical assistance is the transfer of technology and technical know-how, which requires recruitment of mainly indigenous employees at all levels of staffing. How does this happen when most of the manpower used on these projects are expatriates? These kinds of lapses in the negotiation of technical agreements are an indication of inadequacy of leadership, and further proof why incapable leaders need to be kept away from the corridors of power. The old guard must make way for new visionary leaders.

All these gaffes in negotiation notwithstanding, Africa's future is more and more intertwined with Asia, and it is not just Asia, as Russia, Turkey and Iran are replacing the West as major partners of the continent. The World Bank and western bodies like the US Overseas Private Investment Corporation (OPIC) have however realized this and are also becoming more focused on Africa. Who would blame them? Africa's potential for growth is evident for all to see. Despite the seeming slow pace to realizing these potentials, there are several testaments to socioeconomic growth scattered across the continent. We will take time to explore some of these markets in some detail in subsequent chapters. As these partners from the East step into the roles left by former colonizing powers of the West, Africa must be astute in forming these new relationships to avoid getting shortchanged as she was in her colonial and post-colonial past.

It is evident that failures in leadership affect literally all facets of society. Countries with leadership challenges are not able to create the conditions necessary for human capital to be harnessed and thrive. The result is human capital flight in economic refugees and brain drain – the worst kind of human capital flight. This is a situation where the best trained and educated portion of a population chooses to migrate to developed countries due to lack of proper remuneration in their home country. In Nigeria for instance, the health authorities are complaining about reduction in enrollments for both National and West African residency programs. This is not because fewer doctors are qualifying from medical schools, but rather due to their preference for foreign licensing exams. Also, this is happening with professionals from all fields of endeavor, not just doctors. In the end, the developing countries continue to struggle because the young capable hands that should be leading the change are lured to a better life in the developed world – due to no fault of theirs. The blame for this self-destructive trend must be put on the visionless leadership that litters the African landscape. Only the right kind of visionary and selfless leadership can stop this drift.

In the history of every nation, the names of certain leaders stand out for good or for bad depending on the kind of impact they had on their generation, while some others are simply not remembered at all because they literally just marked the roster. Today's African leaders and indeed leaders around the world need to ask themselves what legacies they want to be remembered by when they have departed from this world, and once they decide on one, work tirelessly to leave their mark in the sands of time. The same applies to everyone in any form of authority; be it a father or a council chairman. The transient nature of this life should make us mindful of the legacies we leave behind. An African great encapsulated it perfectly when he said:

"What counts in life is not the mere fact that we have lived. It is what difference we have made to the lives of others that will determine the significance of the life we lead."

Nelson Mandela

CHAPTER 5

DECOLONIZE THE MIND

Sigmund Freud an Austrian neurologist and the founder of psycho-analysis, in his model of the human mind concluded that our minds are divisible into three levels: *conscious, subconscious* and the *unconscious mind*. The conscious mind he theorized was filled with conscious thought; how we perceive an event, trigger a need to react and then depending on the relevance of the event, store it either in the subconscious or uncon-scious area of the mind. The subconscious mind he conceived, held more recent memories which could be recalled quite quickly, such as people's names, recurring thoughts and routine habits and feelings. Thus, he pos-ited that the subconscious mind occupied the most of our brain capacity. Finally, there is the unconscious mind where all our past experiences and memories reside. It is from these deep-seated memories that our belief and value systems manifest and our behaviors, good or bad, are formed.

It is important to note, like I mentioned in my earliest chapters, that these beliefs we hold in our unconscious are acquired over time via our conscious mind. It is in the unconscious mind that we internalize our prejudices and biases. It is also in the unconscious mind that we inter-nalize self-esteem issues and self-defeating beliefs. This unfortunately, is where many colored folks both in Africa and the diaspora find them-selves; in need of detoxifying and decolonizing the unconscious mind.

The mind is the gateway to the human soul. It and our spirit being are about all that sets us apart from other species on this planet. Consequently, if for any reason, the unconscious mind sees nothing but ceilings and barriers (whether real or unreal), and the individual has challenges seeing his or her true potentials, then there is a limit to what an individual in such a situation can achieve. All those nice catch phrases we use like," *possibilities are endless*", "*can do attitude*" and" *impossible is nothing*," become naught when the mind is self-limiting, hence the relevance of this focus area in changing the fortunes of the developing world.

In chapter three, we discussed means by which independent African states could accelerate the reversal of poverty, earn more respect on the global stage and in so doing reverse racism. It is important to point out here that, while many African states officially gained independence from the 1950s through to the 1980s, many of our leaders are still yet to gain mental independence from the West. In this chapter, we continue down the path of how to achieve socio-political emancipation, but with a focus on the intrinsic work of changing our way of thinking.

The most important paradigm shift is again an economic one which has to do with correcting one of many misconceptions that affect our consumption habits, and that is the presumption that only products and services from the West and East are of the finest quality and therefore are preferable to locally produced ones. As strange as it sounds to people unfamiliar with the African continent, patronage of locally made goods and services is a major opportunity area in most African countries. Where the default mindset in most parts of the world is, to patronize locally made products before imported ones, the reverse is the case with most of sub-Saharan Africa.

I have worked long enough in manufacturing and visited many manufacturing plants in different parts of the world to understand that, besides products requiring cutting edge advanced technology; it is possible to produce most basic consumer goods and home and office appliances anywhere in the world. All that is required is the willingness to invest in building the right capabilities, the right technology, and to source the right component materials. Of course, the manufacturing plant's proximity to a sizeable market, the cost structure in that location versus other locations and other supply network design considerations in the end determines which sourcing locations have comparative advantage.

In the end, it is the factors that I highlighted in chapter three, such as poor infrastructure and other handicaps that put Africa at a disadvantage in the cost-value equation as a preferred sourcing location and not some myth about lack of capability. Hence, if an entrepreneur located in Africa can get the right cost-profit mix and has comparative advantage versus imported equivalents of a product, there is no reason he or she cannot match the quality of imported goods and services. Therefore, there is an urgent need to encourage a paradigm shift among Africans towards patronizing locally produced products and services by translating *Import Substitution* from mere written economic policy into living national priorities by rousing consciousness in the developing world.

This is essential in countries like mine where revenues from commodity exports have fueled local appetite for luxurious goods and services in the last couple of decades. This is despite the obvious fact that the fastest way to create mass employment in any nation, especially the developing world, is by producing more of what you "consume", and I use the word *consume* to include services. Agreed, many countries deindustrialise as they grow richer, but It is only when countries have reached certain levels of prosperity that they can afford to deindustrialize, grow their service sectors and source certain goods and services from economies with competitive advantage.

Another dimension to this addiction to foreign products is the brand effect; where consumers ignore the more affordable options (private labels) made in their local markets in preference for foreign brands. People in the developing world need to look more at the value proposition when making choices on what products or services to consume. Agreed, pricey stuff may be of the best quality, but there might be locally produced products of comparable quality for much better price; hence the need to appraise a value equation. A nation which excelled at this was

China which, realizing the size of its market, adopted a protectionist policy that allowed local industry to thrive. Today, the world shops in China. Africa and other developing nations need to borrow a leaf from nations like China and develop their local productive capacities and where there is a need, renegotiate unfavorable trade agreements that allow both cheap as well as expensive foreign products to flood our markets and stifle local production.

It is not enough to rely on import tariffs to discourage patronage of luxurious goods, as consumers with expensive taste are most times willing to pay the premium. Consumers on their part need to be encouraged to consume locally produced products, local services, local entertainment, et cetera. Foreign companies looking to benefit from these markets need to be encouraged to invest in local production, not unlike the US government's policy thrust under Donald Trump. This is part of the written policy in most parts of Africa, but governments need to put more effort into giving life to these policies and making this part of the national consciousness. This may appear protectionist and against the aims and objectives of most trade organizations, but Africa cannot afford to fold her arms and suffer high unemployment rates while her markets guarantee jobs in other parts of the world.

This love for foreign taste does not stop with imported goods and services, as even investment and recreational choices of middle- and higher-income Africans seldom benefit their local economies, thereby leaving the continent short-changed. The typical African wants to spend his holidays in the country of his former colonial powers. The amount of money Africans spend in visa fees, flight tickets and travel expenses to visit these countries is staggering, compared to her per capita income. According to *Statista,* a statistical portal, outbound visitor growth in Africa has been on a steady increase between 2011 and 2018, growing the most in 2016 when it grew by 13.4 percent over the previous year. This is not just confirmation of a budding middle class, but a clear indicator as to where this middle class like to go vacationing; which is outside the African continent.

Our investment choices are not too different with the wealthy preferring to move billions of dollars (sometimes looted funds) to the West and more recently the Middle East. These funds are sometimes stashed in banks who in turn loan the continent back its own monies. It is mind boggling. These are funds which, if invested in African economies, would create jobs and lift millions out of poverty. This is another dimension to misplacement of resources; Africans channeling Foreign Direct Investment into already developed economies. Wealthy Africans favor investing their monies outside Africa. They prefer to acquire assets in the Americas, Europe, Asia and the Middle East, denying Africa of much needed capital and worsening the situation of the continent. Their excuse for this is the stability of these economies.

This could be considered a double whammy; poor countries on the one hand desperate for Foreign Direct Investment, having what little capital that exists in their economies shipped out most times by corrupt leaders looking for safe havens to hide looted funds. This again needs to be made part of the national consciousness. For instance, corrupt leaders with looted funds found stashed in offshore accounts and offshore investments should get stiffer punishment than those with looted funds invested in the local economies, at least until lasting solutions to the endemic corruption can be implemented.

These non-tactical monetary investment decisions are not peculiar to black people in continental Africa. In the United States for instance, statistics show that money in other demographic groups, say Jewish Americans for instance, exchange hands up to eighteen times before leaving the Jewish community while for African Americans, it is probably a maximum of once or even zero time before leaving the black community. Only six percent of black owned money goes back into their community. This is the reason Jews are at the top and blacks are at the bottom of every ladder in American society. Instead of buying Louis Vuitton, Hermes, expensive cars, shoes, houses, dresses, et cetera, blacks should industrialize Africa, build banks and get rid of colonial institutions by putting them out of business.

Entertainment is another sector where minds need to be *decolonized*. I will use sports as an example. Football is literally a religion in Africa and the average young man in sub-Saharan Africa spends his income in support of one European Football Club or the other. Yet we shun our local football leagues to spend what little incomes we have on cable TV rights to European Football leagues which benefit European economies, and then wonder why leagues on the continent do not do so well. I once had a funny encounter with a tow truck driver on the eve of New Year's Eve 2018 in the south-eastern city of Owerri in my country. I had some car trouble and unfortunately in my corner of the world, we do not have Triple A type road side assistance services (a business opportunity for any would-be investors). I managed to find a tow truck driver operating in that neighborhood who, to my surprise, said I would need to give him two hours before he could attend to me. I asked why, and he said he wanted to watch his English premiership team, Manchester United play. Hilarious, isn't it? This fellow was willing to forgo my patronage to watch an English Premier League team play and earn their outrageous wages. I was bamboozled and of course found myself a willing tow truck.

The irony is, this individual's response is actually quite representative of our football-loving African male population; willing to forego business for the pleasure of watching their favorite European football teams play, and yet unlikely to do the same for a local league game. It is not like there is anything wrong with being a fanatical lover of a sports club; after all we all need some way to let off steam. For obvious reasons, if he told me he was willing to forego my business to watch a local team play, I would have seen reason with him, but a foreign team? It did not make patriotic sense.

Unfortunately, this is the reality in Africa; well packaged products from Europe and America overshadowing the home-grown ones to the detriment of the local economy. African FAs (Football Associations) continue to do what they can to get more money into local sports, that way keeping more talent and fans involved in the local league to the benefit of local economies; but as you can see, they are still a long way from attracting enough money and viewership. Of course, there is the other reality that, local leagues cannot grow until local companies do enough business to spend similar amounts of money on local teams as is spent in the developed leagues.

Today, the leagues that do reasonably well enough in Africa are those in South and North Africa, not because these regions have more talent than others but because they have better sponsorship deals for their leagues compared to other regions of Africa. It is common knowledge that West and Central Africa are the repository of raw indigenous African football talent because of our physicality and our African flair. If in doubt, take a look at France's 2018 world cup winning team which was made up predominantly of children of immigrants from these two African sub-regions. Yet our leagues are not popular because they do not have enough funding.

It is not all bad news in entertainment however, as home-grown talents are beginning to take over the musical entertainment scene in Africa. I, for instance grew up in an African metropolis listening to mostly American and British music, and movies, but my children, on the other hand, are growing up listening to African music stars who in the last decade have taken not just the continent but the hip-hop world by storm. African American hip-hop stars who in the past did not want anything to do with stars from the motherland are now looking for collaborations with African stars, and entertainers from the Caribbean are following suit. These struggling music and movie talents from Africa are suddenly much sort brides as minorities in the West continue to yearn for new and fresh content in the music and movie entertainment space. This trend needs to be replicated in sports and other facets of life. Africans need to support African creativity, arts, sports and the local entertainment industry in general.

Clothing and house-hold goods is another sector where this change in consumer behavior is necessary. There is a city in the south east of Nigeria renowned for making quality shoes and clothing. But because of this local preference for foreign brands, these creative local producers end up putting foreign labels on their products in a desperate effort to boost sales. These products are most of the time of similar, if not better, quality than the imported ones, especially those imported from the Far East. Nonetheless, because of the addiction to foreign designer brands, they cannot afford to appropriately label their products *Made in Aba* (the city's name).

If Aba were in Asia or any other part of the world, they would receive government support and by now be earning the economy much needed foreign exchange. But not so in my beloved Nigeria, it has become another sad African story of unexplored opportunity. I am sure every African reading this must have an example of such untapped potential in their individual countries. It is within us all to change these self-limiting habits that keep what little innovation the continent should offer at perpetual infancy. Marketing expertise should be engaged in building African owned brands within Africa first, then outside the continent as time goes on.

This brings me to another area of opportunity in Africa, and that is intra-continental trade which was put at sixteen percent at the time of writing this book. Whereas intra-continental trade in Asia is said to be in the fortieth percentile, Africa does not do enough trade with itself and this can be linked to the low productivity base and overly import-dependent nature of most African economies. Regional trade agreements are not being fully utilized and the only regions showing reasonable trade are the South African Development Community (SADC) and the Pan-Arab Free Trade Area (PAFTA) (can you see any similarity with my earlier embellishment of African Football Associations?).

Once productivity improves, African nations can look across the border more for better deals and cut down on sea freight costs from the Far East and the West. A key enabler to increased productivity will be infrastructure. In West Africa for instance, a trans-ECOWAS highway not far from the Atlantic coast, a standard dual carriage way from Lagos, Nigeria to Abidjan, Cote d'Ivoire (which I have had the pleasure of driving on) is still at different levels of completion, depending on which ECOWAS member state you find yourself driving through. This needs to be supported by Trans regional rail networks across the continent, otherwise sea freights will continue to be cheaper than hauling cargo in-land. Funding for these projects is the first major hurdle that needs to be overcome as many African states struggle with recurrent expenditure and debt servicing, with little left for capital projects.

After funding, there is the small matter of anglophone and francophone antagonism which needs to be overcome. It might sound strange to non-Africans, but in this part of the world, neighbors find it hard to reach agreements because they were colonized by different European states. The major dichotomy is found between those colonized by the English *"God save the Queen"* and those colonized by the French *"Viva la France"*. Sad, isn't it? To think a long-forgotten feud between two European neighbors can be transferred to African countries that have nothing confrontational historically between them begs belief. Cameroon in Central Africa is an epitome of this dichotomy, where the English-speaking West Cameroon is dominated by the larger French-speaking East Cameroon to this day. Our minds in the motherland really need to be decolonized.

This might sound biased but having spent most of my life in sub-Saharan Africa and visited several anglophone and several francophone African nations, there seems to be a sense that francophone African nations have not completely shed colonial ties with the French. You see this in the monetary policies that not only keep their currencies tied to the French franc, but even significant capital flows to and from these countries go through French financial institutions. There is also the *Colonial tax* these African nations still pay to the French for whatever reasons; I like to call it *protection money*. There seems to be an *umbilical cord* still connecting these francophone nations to their former task masters. So much more than the anglophone nations, the French still wield a lot of influence over francophone Africa.

The francophone African nations need to fully free their governments of this influence from the French before focusing on decolonizing their minds. To quote Chimamanda Adichie, a renowned Nigerian novelist in her interview at the *Third Night of Ideas* hosted in France January

2018, "the way anglophone Africans occupy their space in the UK is not the same way francophone Africans occupy their space in France." This differential treatment can be misconstrued as *institutionalized racial discrimination and* may be directly responsible for new social and security problems being experienced there.

Suburbs in different parts of France and Belgium (the ones surrounding Paris are known as the *Banlieues*) have become breeding grounds for increased number of radicalized French minorities willing to carry out horrific terrorist attacks on their fellow countrymen. Racism as much as religious intolerance can be linked to terrorism; nevertheless, I will avoid expounding that link as terrorism is not in the scope of this book. However, to summarize this point, knowing I might offend a few Parisian friends, I think the French can learn a thing or two about letting go of their former colonies from their old neighbor and foe – the British. It is no surprise that the three most vibrant African economies as at the time of writing this book – Nigeria, South Africa and Kenya –are all English-speaking countries. It is imperative that France allows Francophone Africa complete freedom to determine their own futures and be the truly independent states that they are.

Regardless of which European nation colonized the various African states, there is one thing that seems common to these colonial relationships; in the mind of the West, there is this belief that they have some unwritten (almost divine) duty to instruct African states on what to do, as if our leadership are still under some form of tutelage or apprenticeship. Unfortunately, and disappointingly also, many African leaders think they are obliged to accept what these Western nations have to say. Whenever an African leader or a faction in the state emerges less likely to do the bidding of the West, these fellows strangely either meet an untimely end or at best get incarcerated or exiled never to be heard from again. This has been the pattern for the latter half of the last century, but the good news is that even this is changing with new African leadership.

Once again, this pattern of quelling anti-neocolonialist activists in African countries, can be linked to the mindset of these stooges cum leaders and their notion that these colonials *should know better,* which is a delusion rooted in centuries of very effective programming. Hence my conviction that there is need for a decolonization or deprogramming of the mind. It has been said that if you tell a sheep that it is goat for long enough, sooner or later that sheep might start believing it is a goat. That no western nation will compromise, let alone sacrifice, its interests for the interests of any former colony, is a no-brainer. African leaders must learn, not just to do what is in their personal interests, but above all else, must do what is in the best interest of their nations.

African leaders enmeshed in the different conflicts on the continent must realize that personal interests in prolonging conflicts are benefiting only one party, and that is the arms industries in the West and East, because the last time I checked, none of these assault rifles and rocket launchers used in conflicts across the Middle East and Africa are made in the region or by other developing nations for that matter. By allowing these feuds to fester, they are oiling the war machine of the ideological West (as well as the East) with resources that should have be used in laying the foundations for industrialization of their countries. This phenomenon has been described as new or neo-colonialism and might explain why a country like Britain would be looking to leverage its ties with the Commonwealth (where it has greater influence), as it walks away from the European Union (of which it was a founding member).

I certainly hope new African leadership can see through this festering interference and act accordingly, by doing what is necessary. This could be by being more selective of advice from international institutions like the World Trade Organization (WTO) and IMF, or limiting diplomatic relations, and when necessary uprooting moles in their governments engaged in leaking national strategic plans to foreign powers, and other forms of espionage. To be truly independent will take courage, even to the point of being willing to risk losing one's life.

Another effective way former colonies will do well to assert their autonomies is by continuing to shed colonial legacies like colonial names. It is easy sometimes to overlook the importance of a name, but names carry significance beyond just identity. Names have power imbued by both origins and meanings whether you look at it from secular or spiritual points of view. Naming a thing gives the *"Namer"* a kind of dominion over what is named. In the story of creation for Christians and Muslims, Adam's (or Aadam's) task of naming all the animals was an assertion of his dominion over them. Equally of importance is the fact that names had to be changed to signify a rebirth. We can relate with this in the story of Abraham (Ibrahim), who because of his covenant relationship with God changed his name from Abram to Abraham. In the new testament, Simon was renamed Peter by Christ himself as he took leadership of the disciples and Saul renamed Paul before he could start his work of bringing the gospel of Jesus Christ to us, the non-Jewish world.

A name is not to be taken lightly, hence my pleasure when Swaziland's King Mswati III renamed his country eSwatini while I was still writing this book. In 1979, a similar correction was made by Robert Mugabe as he became president when he renamed his country Zimbabwe from Rhodesian. Apparently, they had been named after some Cecil Rhodes who founded a company in that region that made loads of money for the British Empire – can you believe that? Naming a nation after a person who served the crown well, I can think of only one word to describe that –audacious! This reminds me of a story about the longest river in my country Nigeria and the third longest river in Africa – the Niger. Back in my primary school days we were taught that a Scotsman, Mungo Park discovered the Niger River; the very same river my ancestors had been taking dips in for millennia before his *discovery*. Stories like this should not even still be in the school curriculum decades after independence.

Aside from the point of dominion expressed in the renaming of a thing, there is also the perspective of the meaning of names. I come from a culture not unlike many others around the world, that places a lot of relevance on the meaning of names. With newborn for instance, there is usually an intimate connection between the choice of name and "... events which have either direct or indirect bearing upon the birth of the child. Once the circumstances or life history connected with the individual or his parents is known, the name, which may contain a whole story in itself, becomes meaningful." (Wieschhoff 1941) Hence, the role of names in the preservation of identity and culture cannot be overstated.

There is a saying in my mother tongue that goes, "Mgbe onye tere n'úra ka chi foro ya" which means "when a person wakes from sleep is when the day starts for him". Hence, as the massive continent of African awakes (a bit late maybe), she needs to set about fixing things that went amiss while she slept. One of those easy fixes is to remove non-useful colonial legacies like those I have cited above. Asia, the Middle East and Latin America have done and continue to do a great job at this. The Indian sub-continent for instance wasted no time in parting India, Pakistan and Bangladesh into separate countries, and changing names of cities like Bombay to Mumbai. Africa and the rest of the developing world would do well to continue this and systemically dismantle both tangible and intangible colonial influences in our societies, as this will help ramp up national consciousness and pride.

The most effective means of fostering national pride in my humble opinion, is the preservation of indigenous cultures. Apart from customs and traditions, the most important component of culture is language. Language possesses a dual character; in addition to being a means of communication, language is the carrier of culture. A side effect of mass movement of populations across borders to urban areas in globalization and urbanization is the gradual erosion of culture. It is common knowledge that culture (in its undiluted form) is mostly practiced in rural country sides as opposed to big metropolises. Developing nations need to be careful to guard their cultural heritage as they strive to modernize and emulate developed countries of the world. Otherwise, significant portions of their populations will lose more and more of their culture with every passing generation.

I use myself as an example; born and raised in the Lagos metropolis, hundreds of miles away from the place of my parents' origin in the east of the country; one thing I missed out on growing up and sometimes regret is my lack of in-depth knowledge of my native language. Igbo like many African languages is a tonal language, rich in proverbs and idioms which we call "Ilu", not unlike the one I used earlier. Whenever I visit my hometown or the countryside, I enjoy the company of my kinsmen who are experts at using Igbo idioms to make allusions that prompt their listeners to come to the same conclusions without necessarily being explicit. Yet my language is at risk of becoming extinct in the next forty years according to the United Nations Educational Scientific and Cultural Organization; that is of course if adequate steps are not taken to revive it among Igbo children. The UNESCO prediction is clearly an exaggeration, but it serves to exemplify what could become of cultures that do not make the deliberate effort to self-propagate, they will inevitably get engulfed by major ones and become extinct.

I was surprised while doing my research, at the number of languages that have already become extinct; though a good number of them understandably were in North America where a predominance of English and French speakers has phased out the original indigenous tongues in these places. I am not one to speak for the descendants of these indigenous peoples whose languages have fizzled out of existence over time; for all we know it might have been deliberate choices to ease integration into a mainstream and therefore, a welcome development.

That said, this should only be tolerated in countries where these choices on what languages can go extinct and what languages remain are a collective decision of all component ethnicities in such countries. This should not be allowed in developing countries in the name of westernization. Nobody's culture or traditions should be looked upon as inferior or unworthy of propagation as was done during the era of slave trade and colonization. In multi-ethnic societies such as mine, even the smallest minority groups are recognized and encouraged to showcase their unique customs and traditions alongside the major ethnic groups at national events.

It is, however, inevitable that some customs and traditions will eventually fizzle out with modernization and adoption of new religions and even no religion in some instances. The geographical area called Nigeria, for instance, was mostly made up of animists (believers in supernatural powers that organizes and animates the material universe) before Islam with its Arabic traditions took over the north and Christianity with Western values swept through most of the south. Hence, society will inevitably hold on to some customs while letting go of others. However, I do not support the complete erosion of indigenous culture at the expense of modernization or religious beliefs as some indigenous traditions can still find relevance in today's world.

A good African example of how traditional customs can be used to solve today's complex problems, was the role the *Gacaca* community courts played following the tragedy of the Rwandan genocide. In the wake of the 1994 Rwandan genocide, this nation of Africa's great lakes region was faced with the enormous task of trying perpetrators of the genocide. The leaders of the genocide were sent for trial at the International Criminal Tribunal, but the nation's judiciary was left with over a million-ordinary people involved in the crisis who had to be tried. So, the government resorted to a traditional pre-colonial gacaca justice system; twelve thousand community-based courts heard the cases against the foot soldiers of the genocide.

While critics may argue that these trials would eventually strengthen the hold of the Tutsi-dominated ruling party, the Rwandan Patriotic Front (RPF) on the country's politics; they cannot deny the fact that it provided some form of succor and reconciliation to many communities scared by the pogroms. Again, it was the first time these traditional courts would be handling atrocities on this scale, so they can be pardoned for the teething problems encountered with political interference in the process; besides it is sometimes difficult to keep politics out of human affairs completely. Therefore, I am in support of embracing new ways of doing things while holding on to relevant traditions from a people's past.

In the summer of 2018, mainstream media went agog with another high-profile wedding in the British Royal family, when Prince Harry tied the knot with his mixed-race bride, American actress Meghan Markle. Most commentary on the event was centered on the new-found diversity and inclusiveness of the British monarchy which, don't get me wrong, is a very welcome development in that it helps bring down what has become traditional racial barriers. However, I found myself equally (if not more) intrigued by the customs and traditions showcased on that fine Saturday in May which have been in observance for centuries. From the flamboyant royal guards on their horses that escorted the British royals, to the moderation with which the ladies were dressed; the unique traditions of the English with their history were on display at the event.

I am sure every one of Anglo-Saxon ancestry that watched that wedding must have looked on with pride, and I remember thinking to myself, "if a society as open and as tolerant as the British still hold their traditions so dear, then why should any of us be in such a hurry to discard ours so quickly?" In the same vein, developing countries need to put in place policies that balance westernization (or easternization) with the preservation of indigenous cultures because these cultures form part of their identity. Besides, holding on to and being proud of your culture goes a long way in raising national consciousness, decolonizing minds as well as causing other peoples to pay attention, respect and appreciate indigenous cultures of the underdeveloped nations of the world. According to Marcus Garvey, "A people without the knowledge of their past history, origin and culture is like a tree without roots."

I am sure one could find lots of articles and books written about the self-limiting value systems of people from the developing world as the few I have highlighted in this chapter are by no means exhaustive. However, I will mention one more very important point that affects the self-esteem of many colored people and has to do with the world's somewhat flawed perception of beauty. Colored people have been convinced that "Black is not beautiful," and disproving this fable will be the most difficult and arduous of tasks yet. This is the reason why companies centered on beauty products are booming. A thriving multibillion-dollar beauty care industry built mostly around complexion lightening products, hair extensions and cosmetic surgery does not seem to be going anywhere anytime soon; due to colored people's disdain for their dark skin.

If you ask Blacks who are the most beautiful Black celebrities, 9 out of 10 will name the usual suspects like Halle Berry, Beyoncé and Alicia Keys. Celebrities who are either multiracial or those who alter their looks to look more European are seen as more beautiful than others with strong African features. Studies have shown that black people who look more stereotypically black (darker skin, bigger lips, wider noses) tend to be perceived as less attractive than those who look less stereotypically black (lighter skin, thin lips, straight hair) (18 Karat Reggae 2017).

The skin-lightening industry is one of the fastest growing segments of the global beauty industry, particularly in Asia and Africa, with marketing forecasters predicting it will be worth an estimated 31.2 billion US dollars by 2024 (US National Library of Medicine National Center for Biotechnology Information 2018). This is despite a sharp uptick in skin cancer because these products attack the skin's natural protective melanin. It is unfortunate that so many rich skin-toned and curvaceous colored ladies feel the need to alter their complexion to feel more beautiful and appreciated. It is also worth pointing out that colored men are not exempt from this bleaching culture. Those who defend this culture will argue that looking and sounding *white* can be helpful to colored peoples' careers, making it more of a necessity than just a fad. That notwithstanding, as I mentioned earlier, convincing colored people that paleness is nothing to be envied will probably require more effort than would be needed to denuclearize the world. So, I will not waste time by making more than a mention of this aberration.

In conclusion, the effects of centuries of slavery and the close to a century of colonial rule on the paradigms of some colored people will take some years or even decades to fully correct. While many African states technically gained independence in the latter half of the last century, most of them are still yet to gain mental independence from the West and are in some instances, replacing Western colonialists with new ones from the East – in China and Russia. We have erstwhile been taught to value some things that are not necessarily in our best interest and need to dissuade ourselves of these ways of thinking. Whether it is in our choice of where we spend our monies or to whom we seek counsel from, a total top-down realignment of priorities is needed from the upper echelons of power, down to the basic unit of society – the family – across sub-Saharan Africa and much of the developing world. The only thing stopping us, is us. When we change our minds, we change our behavior as well.

Everything, and I mean every little decision pertaining to national policy needs to be vetted with the simple question, "How does this benefit our country?" Because man, by nature is wired to look out for number one – self – before all else. Of course, as I touched on in the previous chapter on leadership, this will depend largely on our ability to flush self-serving politicians out of the corridors of power in our countries and replace them with servant leaders, who have no other interests than that of the people. Only then can there be hope for true decolonization, not just in Africa but in developing nations of the world.

CHAPTER 6

DON'T DESERT THE
MOTHERLAND

In the United States, the month of February is celebrated annually as Black History Month. While this provides a great opportunity, not just for the US but the free world to pause and honor the travails of blacks and other minority groups in their societies, it does not do much by way of truly empowering and bridging the income deficit of most black people much less the fortunes of African nations. African Americans and people of the Caribbean need to take this annual fiesta of commemorative events one step further by doing more than just celebrating black history once in a year. They need to consider re-establishing tangible links with the African continent.

Like other ethnic nationalities in North America, people of African descent should give some thought to channeling more of their time and resources into developing their *homeland*. Agreed, it must be difficult to view a distant continent with which one does not share anything in common besides skin color as a *homeland*, but this can be facilitated if African Americans view the continent as a business opportunity – which it is – and consider investing in it. There are fifty-four nations that make up the continent and with in-depth studies; it should be possible to single out one or two that catch their individual interests.

Up until now most African American interests in the continent have been in tourism, with the historic ports of the transatlantic slave trade on the West African coast and the Wild Life Safaris in East and South Africa being the more popular tourist destinations. But I think this period of stalling growth in the more developed markets of the world is a good time for daring business people to put on their entrepreneurial hats and see the business opportunities begging to be harnessed in Africa. Potential investors among them could schedule a few exploratory visits to markets that interest them and if they are impressed, look for trustworthy local business people who know the terrain to go into partnership with in these countries. Many Chinese, Indian and Arab-owned businesses are already in Africa cashing in on investment opportunities; so, the way I see it, why should our *relatives* on the other side of the Atlantic be left out?

One could write a whole book about countries that owe a lot of their economic prosperity to investments from their nationals that have relocated to other countries. It is common knowledge that a nation like Israel is the major economic and military power it is today because of the support it receives from Jews in the diaspora. The influence which groups like the Israel Lobby have on United States foreign policy is well documented. The most recent dividend of that influence is the US recognition of Jerusalem as the capital of Israel. Need I mention the role Irish-Americans played in Irish independence from the British crown? Throughout the nineteenth century, the Irish-American support took many forms.

From the donation of funds to Irish Fenians, to attacks on Canadian British soil on behalf of Ireland, to moral and financial support from constitutional nationalism and its proponents. In the years surrounding the Easter Rebellion, Irish-America's support continued to play an influential role in the path to an independent Ireland (Cowan 2013).

According to the World Bank's 2018 Migration and Development Brief, even when reviewing global remittances made from high-income countries to low- and middle-income countries which reached a record

$466 billion in 2017 after two previous years of decline, sub-Saharan Africa had the smallest share of $38 billion. East Asia and Pacific had the largest share of $130 billion, followed closely by South Asia with $117 billion, then Latin America and the Caribbean with $80, Middle East and North Africa with $53 billion and Europe and Central Asia with $48 billion.

The Foreign Direct Investment figures published by UNCTAD for 2016 are similar, with FDI inflows into developing economies totaled at $646 billion that year – a 14 percent decline from 2015 – developing Asia received $443 billion, and then Latin America and the Caribbean received $142 billion, while Africa again brought up the rear with $59 billion. (Source: United Nations Conference on Trade and Development UNCTAD, 2017 World Investment Report). Is it a surprise then that sub-Saharan Africa groans under spiraling population figures without matching economic growth to provide opportunities for a teeming youth?

Experts will of course argue that the numbers I shared above are not an apple to apples comparison as for instance; there are much bigger economies in developing Asia versus Africa. Not to mention, the population of developing Asia is double if not triple the African population. However, I believe I made my point; Africa can do with some extra investment.

A 2014 Deloitte report on the investment potentials of sub-Saharan Africa, suggests the key drivers of economic growth in sub-Saharan Africa as: rising household spending and growth in Foreign Direct Investment; growing opportunity for investments in Africa's natural resources: growth of demand in the domestic markets due to rise in the lower middle-class population, and gradual normalization of activities in conflict zones. The fact is you do not need an economist to explain this to you; all the indicators are growing simply because sub-Saharan Africa is starting from a low base. It is similar to economic indicators after a recession; they will almost always be positive because the economy is recovering from a contraction. There is only one direction African economies can and should go, and that is *up*!

In a business meeting with a Lagos based Lebanese business man some years ago, I listened attentively as he spoke frankly as an investor about how the structural barriers to doing business in Africa, such as poor infrastructure, ease of market entry amongst other factors, tend to make Blue Chip Multinationals reluctant to fully commit to investing in Africa. Thus, leaving the space for small family owned businesses, to come in and make handsome returns. Business margins in Africa are not your usually thirty to fifty percent like you are accustom to in developed economies; here businesses target margins a hundred percent and above, depending on the sector.

Everywhere in the world, big corporations have the economies of scale to squeeze small players out of any market, so their lack of commitment in sub-Saharan Africa leaves space for bold small- and medium-scale investors to come in and grow their businesses into empires. The main challenge major corporations' face in Africa is their huge start-up costs. Unlike small businesses who can start small and scale up as their market share grows, multinationals have their *one-size-fits-all* structures for sales, marketing and manufacturing driven by their usual global standardization policies and *best practices*, which make their high running costs unsustainable for small market volumes. Hence, in an effort to meet markets like ours mid-way, they resort to partnering with Small and Medium Enterprises (SMEs).

By being that SME, either already in the market or willing to come into the market for these multinationals, such African American investors would hedge market risks of entry for these multinationals while reaping the high margins they stand to make doing business on the continent. Africa truly is the last remaining unexplored business frontier and African American investors are more than welcome to come *home* and establish their own business empires.

People of African descent in the diaspora need to understand that their reckoning among other ethnic nationalities in their home countries and the racial discrimination they experience is inadvertently connected to the fortunes of African nations. The sooner African and other developing nations begin to take their place in global trade and commerce, the sooner Africans in diaspora will be taken more seriously in their home states. They might not like it, but our fortunes are linked. They can no longer continue to view Africa as "that big old continent out there." They need to begin to understand that Africa is *home*; the motherland as it is often called must be viewed as *home*.

When most Americans think of Africa, the first thing that comes to mind is disease and starving children, not venture capital and startup companies. However, an increasing number of African Americans are venturing to the motherland to develop business relationships and explore economic opportunities. Nigeria, Africa's most populous country and biggest economy, has a burgeoning middle class. According to Canadian newspaper *The Globe and Mail*, there will be 12 million middle-class Nigerians by 2030 (Otiko 2015).

Ever notice the growing number of Africans who now vacation as opposed to migrate, in the United States, Europe and Middle East? They are part of this burgeoning middle-class whom I am proud to be one of. Amanda Spann, an African American partnering on a consultancy with some Nigerian Americans that address key problems that exist for intending African American investors, said she learnt a lot about doing business in Africa when she participated in an innovation tour of several African countries. She writes, "What I noticed while traveling is that African and African-American entrepreneurs often face many of the same challenges. Ultimately, there is no shortage of genius across the African diaspora but entrepreneurs here and there both need access to education, capital and mentorship from stakeholders, who are not only committed to the preservation of these innovators dignity but investing back into their communities."

Although opportunities abound all over the continent, I will not have the luxury of mentioning all of them in this chapter. However, for illustration only, I will now look at the five most populous African nations, their economies and opportunities that lie there-in.

In the heart of Central Africa, the Democratic Republic of Congo (DRC) was ranked 182nd out of 190 countries by the World Bank in its 2018 Ease of Doing Business report, mostly for lack of consistency in its tax legislation and difficulty in accessing utilities such as electricity. However, if you are an investor willing to bet on a commodities boom and more importantly, willing to ignore the political instability, then this market is worth considering. The major minerals being mined in DRC are copper, cobalt and gold.

For perspective, by 2030 global cobalt demand is anticipated to be nearly fifty times higher than what it currently is in 2018, and the Democratic Republic of Congo is home to more than sixty percent of the world's cobalt reserves. While it may not be possible for every business prospector to get directly involved in mining, these projections guarantee that there will be funds available to fuel development in other sectors of their economy. For instance, like disruptors all over the continent, tech innovators and digital entrepreneurs are finding solutions to everyday problems in Congo by offering consumers innovative services.

It is not possible to discuss DRC without a mention of one of the most protracted internal conflicts on the continent which has displaced millions and preoccupied several UN agencies for a prolonged period. The situation has deteriorated to the point that the UN peace keeping force there now acts as local law enforcement; that is the Police. Also, the local currency, the Congolese franc, is so devalued that the US dollar has become the preferred currency for local transactions. Any potential investors should be aware of these risks as the DRC with all its potential is one of the more unpredictable markets in Africa. Although it is hard to find a larger market in the sub-region, investors can consider other markets in Central Africa.

In East Africa, Ethiopia is moving fast on the path to industrialization. Though its key export is Coffee, new industrial parks being built will help boost manufacturing's share of their economy. This country of more than one hundred million has been one of the best performing economies in Africa for the better part of the past decade. Major infrastructural projects are either in progress or in the pipeline. This includes a 6,450 MW hydro-power project and railway lines that will transverse the country due to be built in the coming years. I already mentioned its performing national carrier – Ethiopian Airlines– in an earlier chapter. It is worth mentioning that they have had a few local conflicts the central government is doing well to curtail.

The Republic of South Africa (RSA) also known as the Rainbow Nation is the second largest and most industrialized economy in Africa. RSA with a population of about sixty million benefited from massive Foreign Direct Investment from the Western hemisphere, a result of close ties of previous apartheid governments with the West. Nowhere in sub-Saharan Africa is there a greater need to reverse racism than in South Africa. Since apartheid ended in the early 1990s, the majority indige-nous population, have been working to close the economic gap between themselves and the migrant minority predominantly white population in the apartheid years. This they are doing with their Black Economic Empowerment (BEE) program and land reform policies. South Africa remains the most westernized African economy for any would-be inves-tors and the market with the least number of *surprises* for would-be Western investors. It also has a thriving tourism industry. South Africa is also home to the continent's largest conglomerates.

The Arab Republic of Egypt, with a population of roughly one hun-dred million people is the most populous nation in North Africa and home to one of the seven wonders of the Ancient world - the Great Pyramids of Giza. Egypt's key export is petroleum and crude oil. The Sinai conflict and terrorist attacks presently loom large on their national security and has affected the sizable tourism industry in Egypt. Fewer tourists now visit from the West, but they seem to have been replaced by tourists from Asia – China in particular. Egypt has always been a critical player in the Middle East and a peace broker in the Palestinian – Israeli conflict. Gulf countries have helped Egypt to cushion some of the impact of its 2016/17 economic crisis, by paying cash to their central bank. The Saudis were as at the time I was compiling this book, proposing a five hundred-billion-dollar industrial zone that would link their country to Egypt and Jordan. Another big economic boost was in the offing in their power sector, as three new 4.8 GW power plants and twelve wind farms under construction will definitely double the country's electricity production to 16.4 GW. Egypt also has huge gas deposits, the largest in the Mediterranean.

Last and by no means the least, Nigeria is the most populous black nation on the planet with a population of roughly one hundred and eighty million people. Like Egypt, Nigeria's key export is Petroleum and crude oil, though this now accounts for some fifteen percent of her economy – the largest in Africa. Like most nations, Nigeria's greatest potential is its people. A study carried out in the United States revealed that African immigrants in general reportedly earn up to thirty percent more than US born blacks, and Nigerians are the highest earning and most educated of these African immigrant populations in the country.

Nigeria is not free of conflicts as in the last five years it has witnessed the rise of what has become the deadliest terror group in the world – Boko Haram, which is another instance of mismanaged internal strife. The Nigerian state literally weaponized Boko Haram by trying to violently crush what was originally just a minor religious sect. The Nigerian authorities created a full-blown rebellion out of what was a small group of extremists kicking against elitist misrule. Their activities are however restricted to the north of Nigeria and northeast in particular, where they occasionally commit suicide attacks and engage the military in skirmishes. Boko Haram has turned into a tool in the hands of politicians, the old type of politicians who still use sectarianism as a means to achieve their selfish objectives. But I am convinced that once sincere leadership can find its way into government, it will only be a matter of time before funding ceases to these kinds of sects.

Nigeria's most populous city and my home – Lagos – has grown into a Tech hub and a huge market for Asian Tech companies. Necessity, they say, is the mother of invention and our market, where capital and infrastructure constraints should be hampering growth have become fertile ground for innovation. An example is in Fintech (Financial Technology) where fresh improvisations in mobile technology are turned out regularly. In entertainment, Nigeria and Ghana are famous for their low budget, yet highly successful film industries. The music industry also based in Lagos has become a billion-dollar industry with a large fan base all over as well as outside the continent.

Having said that, I believe the greatest opportunity for Nigeria, lies in its manufacturing sector. With such a huge market, still dependent on imported goods and services, growing the local manufacturing base to deliver import substitution and much needed jobs for a teeming youth population is its shortest route to prosperity. Yet challenges of decades of mismanaging its electricity grid (under a prolonged military era), means businesses need to invest in gas and diesel generators. Power costs companies in Nigeria at least thrice as much as in developed countries. This coupled with other infrastructure challenges makes local manufacturing cumbersome and drives up production costs. However successive governments since the return to civilian rule in 1999 continue to spend billions of dollars to bridge the gap between demand and supply of power.

Each of these fore mentioned countries is leading economic growth in their respective regions; Central Africa, East Africa, South Africa, North Africa and West Africa respectively. Whether they and other African nations succeed will depend on Africa's ability to maintain political stability and stay conflict free, while working to realize its world-renowned potential. Should Africans in diaspora hedge their bets and invest in Africa? Certainly! Business opportunities abound in Africa. Their fortunes in their part of the world more than anyone else's, is linked directly and indirectly to Africa's. Hence, they owe it to themselves and their children to *bring back* whatever expertise they have gathered and whatever capital they can spare and invest in Africa. Yes, you read me right, I said *"bring back"*, because they are Africans, as African as Kunta Kinte of the world-famous Mandinka village. We are bound by thousands of years of shared ancestry, a common struggle for economic emancipation and a universal gift of rhythm.

One of the main selling points of the African market is that there is still a lot of white space markets. I mean from the simplest consumer goods like shower gels (as most of the continent still use bar soap) to the more capital-intensive sectors like power. Nigeria for instance, still has a 160,000 MW power shortfall to meet national electricity demands, with similar opportunities scattered across the continent and the projections continue to increase as you look farther into the future. Also, unlike the developed world, there are still ample investment opportunities in consumer essentials such as health, agriculture and housing. These are sectors where returns on investment are almost guaranteed anywhere in the world. In the health sector, the major opportunity areas are in equipment and facilities, as many of the continent's hospitals still make do with old medical equipment. The shortfalls in health have made the wealthy in African society resort to medical tourism in Europe, North America and India. Whereas, if more private hospitals are able to provide these health services, set-up in the continent, fewer middle- and upper-income families will see need to fly abroad for medical treatment.

In the agricultural sector as mentioned previously, a majority of African farmers are still predominantly into subsistence farming, sometimes with constrained fertilizer supply; meaning the industry still has plenty of room for investors with proven methods of increasing crop yield. Similarly, most livestock breeders still use outdated animal husbandry techniques, such as open grazing for cattle instead of ranching, not to mention the breeds of livestock being reared which are not the higher yielding types. It will be hard to believe that because of this lack of ranches and high yield cattle breeds; a nation the size of Nigeria for instance, still imports one hundred percent of its dairy needs. A market of over one hundred and eighty million consumers; that is any investors dream, isn't it? Agribusiness in African is a gold mine with investors almost guaranteed good returns as the continent strives for food sufficiency. Allow me to furnish you with a few exciting facts about agribusiness in Africa.

Africa's richest man, Aliko Dangote, recently invested $1 billion in rice production, which makes a lot of sense considering that every year; Africa spends billions of dollars importing rice.

Also, since 2009, investors in the USA, Europe, Middle East and Asia have been buying and leasing millions of hectares of African land for agriculture. Unknown to many people, there is a serious trend of land grabbing by foreign interests for African land. Foreign Direct Investment in African agribusiness in 2010 alone was $10 billion and is projected to reach $45 billion by 2020. Agriculture is taking a huge leap in Africa and investors want a piece of the action too. It is projected that Africa's agribusiness industry will be worth $1 trillion by 2030! That's huge! If this projection by the UN comes true, agribusiness will become the 'new oil' in Africa!

In the light of all these facts, one is tempted to ask, how come the rich and wealthy folks are investing in Africa's agribusiness industry while the majority of Africans are largely ignorant about the amazing potentials of agriculture on the continent? So, for investors looking to start a business or invest in an industry that makes a significant social impact, provides jobs and creates sustainable wealth, agribusiness in Africa is surely the way to go.

Much of West, East and Southern Africa have developed National Agriculture and Food Security Investment Plans (NAFSIPs) which investors can tap into and cash-in on the continent's agricultural transformation drive. In the area of health and nutrition, Africa's capacities in research and development are improving, with Regulatory Centers of Research Excellence (RCOREs) established all over the continent, however funding for research is understandably still not yet where it should be.

In the real estate sector, the housing deficit is quite high on the continent, the gory images of poor slums main stream media have come to associate with Africa and other developing markets makes this quite obvious. Real estate developers able to provide simple, affordable housing solutions for lower- and middle-income families are making a fortune in markets across the continent and the developing world.

Real estate remains a booming opportunity for Africa-focused investors for good reasons. The growth of Africa's cities creates a demand for increased volumes of high-quality commercial and residential real estate. The rise of the urban middle-class drives retail property development, particularly as modern shopping malls spread across the continent. A growing number of multinational companies are searching for office space in the emerging cities. Africa's population boom is also a burdening factor on Africa's cities. A need for mass market affordable housing, high-end properties and all in-between, stems from the diversity in the multiplying populations, including middle to high-income locals (Davis 2015).

The six-emerging real estate investment hotspots in Africa are; Abuja Nigeria, Naivasha Kenya, Casablanca Morocco, Jardins de Carthage Tunisia, Ndola Zambia and Algiers Algeria (Mulupi 2015). So, in summary, the message is there are lots of viable real estate investment options on the continent which foreign real estate investors can explore.

On business equity, most African nations generally assure one hundred percent foreign ownership of most investments, with exception of sectors covered by local content and Cabotage Acts (related to coastal and in-land water transportation). Many also have legislation on non-expropriation of investment, which essentially protects enterprises from being nationalized or expropriated by government. A typical would-be investor might be concerned about business sustainability and the security of investment. The continent has been on the receiving end of unfavorable press for decades, which does not help build investor confidence.

However as more of the continent continue with sector reforms to put their economies on sound-footing while strengthening democratic institutions; Africa now has success stories of sustained economic and political stability after eras of autocratic rule. In an earlier chapter I gave examples of nations like Ghana in West Africa, Tanzania in the east of the continent and South Africa that have made significant progress on the journey of political stability. To that list I can add, Senegal in West Africa, Kenya in East Africa, Botswana and Zambia in Southern Africa. It is no surprise that two of the more politically stable countries are among the top three economies on the continent – South Africa and Kenya. In addition to these, most African countries have moved on from the era of military rule. Even the few countries still governed by sit-tight presidents are managing sustained socioeconomic growth.

Fiscal incentives, such as tax holidays for activities classified as Pioneering and Capital Allowances exist for certain sectors, and as much as all these are done to encourage capital inflow to our markets, we equally try as much as possible not to interfere in the outflow of capital also. For investors who need to repatriate profits and dividends (net of taxes of course); Africa is one of the easiest places to repatriate profits from. In fact, it has become too easy as multinationals are reported to take advantage of this in short-changing the continent on taxes as well. Africa losses about 200 billion US dollars annually to profit repatriation and tax avoidance.

There are several Grow Africa Initiatives sponsored by both private and public institutions around the continent. Readers can connect with these for more information as I cannot delve deep into every single investment opportunity on the continent. Also, each country typically has an Investment Promotion Commission or its equivalent available, from which potential investors can get more market specific details.

People of African descent in diaspora and indeed the developed world, need to make a deliberate concerted effort to invest in the African continent; not just because it is the profitable thing to do, but also as a means of restitution for centuries of the continent's neglect. There was a time in the eighteenth century when the economic strength of the United States was built on *free* slave labor, therefore America cannot deny the part African Americans played in making the United States the economic giant it is today. Similarly, European economies would not be what they are today had it not been the lopsided trading and resources taken from Africa when she was under colonial and more recently, neo-colonial administrative structures.

The moral angle aside, despite all the centuries of getting short-changed, Africa remains a major pool of human and material resources, with vast potentials yet to be fully harnessed. To be honest, at times, I choose to look on the bright side of Africa's underdevelopment. How? I will explain. I see developing economies like those in Africa as being advantaged in the sense that they have forerunners in the more developed economies of the world from which they learn. The advantage of having forebears is that, if you are wise, you can learn from their mistakes; you can leverage their hindsight and avoid unnecessary iterations – hindsight is 20/20 vision. Although I will be the first to admit that what works in one region of the world is not guaranteed to succeed in another and vice versa; nevertheless, developing economies should be able to look at the experiences of developed and transition economies (those changing from socialist-type central planning to free market economies), and learn from their successes as well as their mistakes.

For example, in environmental sustainability, developing economies have the benefit of seeing the long-term effects of fossil fuels on the environment, and can take advantage of technological advancements in alternative energies and begin now to invest in renewable energies. So, we have an opportunity to stand on the shoulders of developed countries and avoid their learning curves as some nations in the Middle East, Central and Southeast Asia are doing; if, and only if, we can get past the things that divide us, and focus more on things that unite us. In the end, there is no better time than now for emigrated Africans to look *homeward* and see how they can play a part in this African renaissance because whether they choose to be part of it or not, Africa is on the rise.

A first step in this direction would be for these investors of African descent to get to understand the uniqueness of the various identities on the African continent, start to refer to individual countries by their names, and stop joining the rest of the world in clustering Africa's various countries into one. Once they overcome this, they can choose to go a step further to understand and sign onto Pan-Africanism and the African Renaissance. Then, with their hearts firmly rooted in the *cause*, they can begin to look at which ways they can use their skills, resources and networks to draw more attention to opportunities as well as challenges which they can make an impact in, in the motherland. I read somewhere that *the quality of a man's life is not measured by how many breaths he takes, but rather by how many breath-taking moments he inspires.* There is no better time than now for Africans all over to get involved in Africa.

In summation, once the remaining African states still struggling with one form of internal strife or the other can get on top of their game, like a couple of peaceful nations on the continent have already done; Africa's potential for a better future is bold and bright and is centered on the convergence of sustained economic progress, rapid urbanization, and tech-savvy youths across the continent. As it stands on the cusp of vast economic and social growth, the African continent at present is only scratching the surface.

CHAPTER 7

SEIZE THE NARRATIVE

Right from the days when early Man would gather around fires at night (in the more temperate regions of the world) and under the moonlight (in the more tropical regions), mankind has always loved a good story. A good storyteller in the village almost always emerged an opinion-molder as well as an Influencer in the community. This the storyteller did by literally influencing the decisions and behavior of his or her listeners and eliciting a desired response out of them. This is as true today as it was back then. Nowadays, these influencers are better known as Opinion Leaders.

Today's stories are however, being told via the media which has become a powerful force in contemporary society, and which determines our actions and even our identities. The power of modern media began to take on a life of its own at the start of the twentieth century, with the development and growth of new mass media technologies. Along with this came increased sophistication of persuasion "professionals," who would use war propaganda for instance, as early as in World War I to whip up nationalist sentiments and manipulate emotions towards war to good effect back then, and in every other war ever since.

An incident shortly after the introduction of another mass media technology – the radio – occurred in the United States, when H.G. Wells' book, *War of the Worlds* aired on Halloween eve 1938.Then one of the earliest fictional productions of extraterrestrials invading earth, aired on radio and led to mass panic and hysteria; even the broadcasters must have been surprised by its *success*. The incident must have opened the eyes of leaders and opinion molders, to the realms of possibility new means of mass communication were making plausible back then. History has since shown us similar spheres of influence that accompanied other break-through mass communications technologies like television, the internet, mobile phone technology and most recently, social media, where literally anyone can now propagate his or her own agenda.

Society relies a great deal on technology for news, entertainment and education. Mass media is seen as one of the greatest influential factors on the opinions and viewpoints of society in the modern world. Media includes a range of sources for example, magazines; internet; television; books and radio. All these sources are what contribute to the beliefs of what society believe life and culture to be, which is sometimes heightened to unrealistic standards. Although media provides speedy access to various forms of communication, as with anything else, negative ones closely follow its positive attributes (studymoose.com 2016).

As such, despite the innumerable wonderfully positive things media has been used to achieve in the last century, media has, is and continues to be used to perpetrate many wrongs in our societies to this day, including racism. While discrimination and marginalization may take place in normal social interaction such as everyday public discourse, it is those groups who are in control of most influential public discussions, that is, *symbolic elites* such as politicians, journalists, scholars, and writers, that play a significant role in the spread of dominant knowledge and ideologies in society. Since prejudices are not innate, but socially acquired, and since such acquisition is predominantly discursive, the public discussions of the symbolic elites are the main source of shared ethnic prejudices and ideologies.

By this logic of the role of the *symbolic elites* and of public discourse, the mass media play a prominent role in the reproduction of racist social representations. Even if politicians sometimes have the first word on ethnic issues, for instance in parliamentary debates, their discourses and opinions become influential only through media accounts. Scholars and writers may publish books and articles, but the main results of these studies become part of the public domain only when reported and popularized in the news media. In sum, the media are currently the most influential source of racist bias, prejudice, and racism (Dijk 2012).

This brings us to the fifth means of reversing racism which, in my opinion, works hand in hand with decolonizing the mind and loving one's own heritage. It is the next step as it involves undoing distortions caused by decades of unchecked maligning of ethnic minorities in the West. It will not necessarily require revisiting every single misconception planted in people's minds with the intention of redressing them; on the contrary, it will require exposing and *selling* positive things that are indigenous to these minority groups, by retelling their stories. In the case of Africa, it means retelling the African story along with that of the rest of the underdeveloped world. To be fair, several mainstream media corporations have begun doing this already, but their efforts do not have the desired intensity and could be mistaken as half-hearted. In certain instances, the intent seems to be to massage egos of colored people for past wrongs with what can best be described as "politically correct content."

An indigenous society's story is best told by its people and in case of the African story, by Africans; that is either African owned media houses or unfettered Africans working in these big media corporations. The reason I say this is, inasmuch as it is not written in the ethics of journalism, it is sometimes important for a journalist to – in the first place – believe the information he or she is reeling out to listeners, and this is easier when these journalists can themselves relate with the stories they report. Occasionally when watching non-colored anchors report on colored stories, it can be so easy to spot subtle expressions and nuances in their spoken and unspoken communication that communicate a lack of conviction when reporting stories on minorities. Hence, my preference to hear our stories from reporters with a genuine love for the people they are reporting on. There is a need for more African investors as well as professionals to step into the media space, seize the narrative and tell the African story.

Media is power, and whoever controls media in a nation as well as the continent, wields power. Africa needs to tell its own stories and stop leaving the rest of the world to tell it on her behalf. A major move in this direction would be for those that create content in media houses, including producers and creative writers to deliberately change the African narrative. Our media houses for instance, do not have to amplify every negative story that comes out of the continent. There are equally negative things that happen in the West as well as the Far East that do not get disproportionate news coverage in mainstream media. Stats on gun related violence and serial killings in North America are astounding, yet even when these figures do make the headlines and front pages, they are not usually over emphasized; until of course recently, that mass shootings have strengthened the call for gun control. Why is this? Because governments through the media deliberately tone down these kinds of news so as not to adversely affect the local economies where these incidents occur, as well as the *brand equity* of the State and Nation. The fact that none of the major cable news and entertainment companies are owned by Africans does not help either.

However, this trend is changing as more and more private media companies open and enjoy increasing viewership from citizens bored of half-truths peddled by State owned media. Governments need to provide incentives to ensure the few African cable news and entertainment companies in operation not only remain in business but grow to eventually compete on the global stage. Having said that, Western media corporations such as the British Broadcasting Corporation (BBC) must be given some credit for their broadcast services in indigenous languages of Commonwealth member states. These BBC services in other languages including African languages are an avenue for people to tell their stories and it has been used to good effect for the last five to six decades. In addition, it helps propagate indigenous languages among the youth.

The intent should not be to suppress negative stories coming out of Africa. On the contrary, it should be more about not dwelling on them as much. Unpleasant bulletins instead should be communicated with non -condescending language, while positive ones such as stories on tourism, industry, creative arts, seasonal festivals and the rich and diverse cultures coming out of the continent and black communities should be deliberately showcased more often. A quote that encapsulates this theme well is one by an author Mwalimu K. Bomani Baruti, "I will never use derogatory, demeaning language against my Brothers and Sisters. I will always show them the utmost respect. I will speak to them in the race-nation spirit of family, knowing that we are one and that to curse them is to curse myself."

Stories of black history need to be told more often. Many people of African descent know more about Western history and culture because that is the history that documentaries on television focus on, not to mention major Hollywood epic blockbuster movies. Gallant tales of the likes of William Wallace of Scotland, King Richard the Lion Heart and the Duke of Wellington of England are too well known by people of color, yet many have never heard of African Kings and Queens who did exploits. Some examples of these renowned Africans include: King Hannibal of Tunisia who confronted and defeated the Roman Army in battle; also King Mansa Musa a wealthy man who established expansive trade routes and influenced the world-renowned University of Timbuktu; Shaka, the Zulu King who united South African tribes against European colonial rule; Yaa Asantewa who after British attempts to loot Ashanti artifacts in Ghana, rallied an army to fight off the British; Amenhotep IV of Egypt famous for promoting Monotheism a thousand years before Christianity.

Other prominent Africans include, Taharqa, the ruler of Napatan Kush who recaptured Egypt from Assyrian occupation. Many people do not know that the original rulers in Egypt, the Pharas were not even Arabs. In fact, they were dark skinned and originated from south of present-day Egypt towards Sudan. I learnt this first hand on one of my many visits to Egypt. Queen Nzingha of Angola a female warrior, fought off Portuguese slave traders from her lands for thirty years. Zumbi dos Palmares, a great Brazilian warrior figure who led a massive slave resistance in the 1600s. Lastly, but definitely not the least, Mekeda of Ethopia, popularly known as the Queen of Sheba and her collaboration with King Solomon, well documented in the Bible.

Stories need to be told of African kingdoms that existed Before Christ's Era such as, the Ife, Nok, Akan and Wagadu Mande of West Africa; the Kush, Medjay, Punt and Da'amat of East Africa; and the Himba, San, Luba-Bemba and Mwari-Nguni of South Africa. These were great kingdoms that existed in the era of the Assyrians, Persians and the Greeks. Africans need to seize the narrative and project more of our under-reported heritage. Agreed, these kingdoms did not go out to capture territory and colonize other peoples, but they were well-organized societies for their time.

In the United States of America, the roles of colored people who worked and fought alongside the American founding fathers in their war of independence against the British are equally under-reported. Among them were the likes of, Peter Salem of Massachusetts who as a slave, fought and saved scores of his white comrades in 1775 at the battle of Bunker Hill during the American Revolutionary War; Prince Whipple who fought alongside George Washington during the American Revolution; James Armistead another slave who served the Continental Army during the American Revolution and gave the revolutionaries plans of the British colonials by being a double agent; Lemuel Haynes was a Pastor and the first African American to receive a Master's degree. He preached a special sermon to his commander-in-chief (George Washington) yearly on his birthday; and Benjamin Banneker was an astronomer and mathematician who was inspirational in the eighteenth century and frequently described as the first African American man of science.

It is important to note that, these great men accomplished these feats in very segregated societies where, at a point slaves had to learn how to read and write in hiding to avoid the wrath of their owners. Similar stories can be told of exploits of African trail blazers in the United Kingdom and the European mainland, including Olaudah Equiano who was captured at age eleven as a slave from the South East of Nigeria and after serving aboard slave ships and British navy vessels, purchased his freedom in 1766 and settled in England where he worked tirelessly as an abolitionist and author the rest of his life.

For centuries, the role of these and other great Africans in the founding of America and the fight against slavery have remained largely untold. As if that was not bad enough, the narrative from early encounters of western voyagers with Africa did not help as they portrayed Africans as almost a sub-human race. Words like *savages* were wrongly used to depict Africans, Asians, and Native Americans by European explorers, whose tales of greed and ruthlessness are only now beginning to emerge.

Fortunately, enlightenment makes us know today that these initial parodies were largely born out of ignorance and the old human habit of belittling what we do not understand. We now know that this was very far from the truth, as these civilizations not only traded precious commodities with their European visitors; they had the most magnificent works of art which were eventually taken from them and are still on display in museums in the West. Savages could not possibly have been able to create such works of art, only civilizations could have done that. Not to mention that some of these civilizations were as old as and at times even older than western civilization. Sub-Saharan Africa can only be guilty of not making major contributions to Science and Technology, but even this (like I explained previously) can be linked to our lack of ambition in warfare. Historians have always confirmed a direct link between innovations for warfare and technological advancement in the last millennia. This means that lack of military ambition by early African empires in part is responsible for the lack of advancement in technology historically.

Africa and people of color generally, need rebranding – a total image overhaul – because mainstream media and the movie industry have not been fair to people of color. They have for centuries deliberately and subconsciously built up whites as the source of most that is good in society and blacks (and colored people) as the source of most that is bad, when the reality is that, this is very far from the truth. We all know how the world of Math would have been limited by the quite cumbersome Roman numerals had it not been for the Arabic numerals we use today. Also, very few people know that Coffee, one of the most widely used mental stimulants, originated in Ethiopia. I can go on and on with examples of numerous other contributions from the East to science and the humanities.

In the United States for instance, this subconscious programming of whites as the progenitors of all that is good plays out in the dominance of Caucasian lead characters in Hollywood blockbuster movies. Conversely, the image of blacks as being no-good burdens on society plays out in motion pictures that portray black men as drug dealers and users and mostly absentee fathers from their children's lives. However, in reality, it is the system of institutionalized racism that makes it appear blacks are the main perpetrators of these negative kinds of behaviors. For example, the US criminal justice system has law enforcement agents engage in selective scrutiny of blacks compared to other demographics. According to a report by Humans Right Watch, there are close to five times more white drug users than black ones in the United States (which makes sense considering blacks are a minority), yet African Americans find themselves incarcerated at several times the rate whites are incarcerated for drug related offences. The system all together makes blacks less likely to succeed and the media in particular has played a lead role in propagating these unflattering stereotypes.

I once stumbled upon a video online published by the *Awareness News Report* in which researchers sampled Caucasian, Hispanic and African American children by placing pictures and dolls of white, brown and black babies before them and asking them which dolls they associate with smartness, goodness, prettiness, badness, ugliness and meanness. Their responses were unanimous; astonishingly, even the black kids associated the black dolls with badness, ugliness and meanness and associated prettiness, goodness and smartness with the blue-eyed white dolls. That can best be described as "deep conditioning". The research proves how rigged and unfair the system is towards colored people and illustrates how images children are exposed to from an early age already predisposes them to racist and deficiency mindsets, even before they are old enough to discover things for themselves and form their own opinions about people.

As mentioned in earlier chapters prejudices are not innate, but socially acquired, and this is even worse when acquired by innocent children. From an early age these kids are denied the opportunity to draw their own conclusions about people and instead biases are forced on them from watching the media and adults around them cast aspersions on certain ethnic groups. With children, these aspersions come in the simplest things, like the cartoon characters they grow up watching, and which characters were predominantly heroes and what characters were predominantly evil villains. Until recently, I did not even realize that there were no major black comic book heroes until all the buzz about the *Black Panther* movie when it premiered in February 2018.

It is bad enough that this has gone on for centuries unchecked and could take many decades to correct. But to see a few African owned media houses and movie production companies that have emerged, still suffering from the brainwashing of institutionalized racism, to the point that they join mainstream media in tainting the black image –by continuing the portrayal of negative stereotypes in their TV shows and news bulletins is disheartening. This is not good enough and only confirms how effectively they have been programmed by a biased mainstream. This should not continue and must be reversed, urgently.

The acquisition of black magazines like Ebony and Jet which had for decades made it their mission to chronicle African-American life, by a Texas based private equity firm in 2016 along with other similar high-profile acquisitions, lent credence to the fear that black-owned media was suffering a slow death in the United States. Timuin in a Detroit IP TV online publication noted that, "Blacks own less than one percent of full power commercial television stations and less than three percent of commercial radio stations yet make up nearly 14 percent of the total U.S. population." The major reason for this is the lack of advertisers that do not target black and minority communities, which is why more of these black-owned businesses would be wise to move more towards the mainstream while retaining their black content. This should not be as difficult today as it was a few decades ago, because more and more non-blacks are proponents of diversity and inclusion in different facets of society and are increasingly beginning to enjoy content which in the past would have appealed mostly to people of color. This broadening of audience and customer base is essential for survival because in a competitive market, the size of a business cannot be ignored.

For media companies on continental Africa the competition seems to be more between state owned and privately-owned media companies. This of course is less prominent in some markets compared to others. In South Africa, for instance, private owned media dominate because they have more press freedom. Many African media houses, unfortunately, neglect their core responsibility of keeping the public informed to dance to the tune of politicians for a quick buck. Despite their designated role of unbiased reporting, mainstream media are businesses first and foremost and occasionally are for hire. This, however, is not a problem peculiar to Africa or developing countries for that matter, as recent polarized elections in the West have reminded us the extent to which the media can take sides in politics. But the problem with African media seems to be one of misplaced priorities as the majority of African journalists seem more concerned with international news bulletins beamed by mainstream media and hardly give enough airtime to local news stories that are equally deserving of coverage. If we do not tell our own stories, who will?

I recall in the 30 months or so that I lived in Kent in the south east of England while doing my master's degree, how the only images I ever saw of Africa were either stories of one conflict or the other, or when charities like Oxfam advertised for donations to help *starving people* in the developing world. Yet this is so far from the realities on ground amongst the majority in these countries. In an earlier chapter when I narrated my less than pleasant encounters with immigrations in Europe and Asia, those officials responded to me based on a stereotype they had formed about people from my part of the world. These stereotypes were the result of a generalization that if Mr. X is from Country Y and there are stories of people from Country Y being behind many internet fraud schemes, then there are high chances that Mr. X is an internet fraudster. Meanwhile, the persons involved in these schemes may represent less than 0.001 percent of the population.

Every so often when I am back home, I would run into expatriates on the continent who admit that if more people in the West could get past the travel advisories and gory images they see about developing countries and experience these places for themselves, their impressions would be much different, and the world would be a very different place in their eyes. Little wonder some people in the West occasionally ask immigrants some of the most patronizing questions. Like *if we have wild life in our cities back home?* Probably born out of the impression that the continent is one big Safari. The fact is, they do not know better because their media have not given them that choice.

For instance, it is hard to believe that some people in the West – including the former Vice President of the United States Joe Biden – have been on record as referring to Africa as a country in this twenty-first century. If liberals can make this kind of mistake, then I do not even want to imagine what to expect from conservatives. Biden's gaffe aside, a lot of the world is guilty of treating Africa as a monolithic country, instead of the continent of fifty-four distinct sovereign nations that it is. This habit of bunching the continent up happens more often than not when the news coming out of one or two of its sovereign members is not good. If there is an Ebola outbreak in two or three African countries for instance, then all Africans in all thirty million square kilometers of her massive land mass suddenly become potential carriers.

It is not possible to underestimate the power of the media today. In these modern times, media has unparalleled influence on all aspects of human life; especially when it comes to shaping popular opinion. A whole lot of people, some of whom I know, have decided altogether not to listen to the news anymore, because they worry that the media are now so adept at propaganda and cannot be trusted anymore. If this proficiency at deploying agendas had remained with conventional media, (i.e. newspapers, magazine, radio and television) it might have been bearable and even possible to curtail their excesses by one means or the other. Unfortunately, the plurality enabled by social media has made it almost impossible to curtail the preponderance of fake news. In fact, it has leveled the playing field so much that, both pros and amateurs are now able to misinform the public at will for little or no cost. On social media for instance, to ensure their posts get the most hits, fake newsmongers come up with the most intriguing and eye-catching captions that make it literally impossible for users to scroll past. The captions are sometimes so intriguing that social media users share these articles before they even read them. I have occasionally come across some of these eye-catching posts, and on examining them, discovered they were less beguiling and even sometimes unrelated stories. I think it was Winston Churchill who fittingly said, "A lie gets halfway around the world before the truth has a chance to get its pants on."

Misinformation that has fed racist ideology for centuries is a bit different from the modern age fake news we have grown accustomed to. It is different because the stories are not entirely made up, but rather unpleasant stories about ethnic minorities, cherry picked for the sole purpose of belittling a people, deflating their self-esteem and making them think less of themselves. Despite the saying that bad news sells papers, mainstream media has been guilty of playing down positive stories and encouraging images coming out of these minority communities and developing countries in preference for less flattering and prejudiced ones. Some of this biased reporting have become so habitual that the media no longer realize that this reportage is actually "implicitly biased", as it fuels racial and religious bias among unsuspecting consumers of their news, education and entertainment, who subconsciously acquire these social prejudices. In other words, even the media has been "deeply conditioned" to be racially biased.

The good news is that these misleading analyses of minority communities and countries is constantly being identified and getting pulled off the air waves, which is the least we can expect considering it has been half a century since the United Nations International Convention on the Elimination of All Forms of Racial Discrimination was adopted in 1965 and entered into force four years later in 1969. Like an onion, it is taking some time to peel back layer after layer of racial discrimination which for centuries, was painstakingly enshrined as part of culture to guarantee white supremacy which today has been watered down to white privilege. The first step to fixing any problem is acknowledging a problem exists and many media houses are realizing that there is some bias in their reporting. These corporate media houses are taking steps such as, examining the sources of their stories because to portray issues fairly and accurately, media must broaden their spectrum of sources. Others are looking at their race and gender diversity compared to the communities they serve. One of the advantages of having diversity in a workforce is that you avoid double standards by ensuring that demography's affected by an issue have a voice in its coverage – a point I made earlier in the chapter.

It is important for the developing world to continue to leverage the power of the media, both conventional and nonconventional media, to correct the mislabeling of the past. The consensus agenda must continue to be rectifying damage already done by decades of misinformation by mainstream media. As I mentioned earlier, the best way to do this is to focus on the positive stories coming out of minority demography's and the developing world, as opposed to engaging in confrontational tit-for-tat and responses to negative stereotypical rhetoric in the media. To borrow the words of a former first lady of the United States, Michelle Obama, "When they go low, we go high."

There are so many breathtaking things to see in the developing world, whether it is natural sceneries and wild life, man-made architectural wonders, historical landmarks or traditional festivals; there are so many tourist destinations deserving further development that should be showcased to the world. The developing world is also littered with business success stories and entrepreneurial achievements, which show that despite structural challenges and humble beginnings, dreams are still being achieved in these parts of the world. One cannot begin to capture how far these positive stories and images go in rectifying the wrong perceptions the West have about people from the developing world.

I recall, on my first trip out of Africa, to England in 2004 for my master's degree, I started up sharing accommodation with two English girls who were quite pleasant and lots of fun. However, one of them hinted to her parents that she was sharing a flat with a Nigerian *fresh* from Africa. In a panic, her parents flew down from the midlands to Kent the next weekend to see this Nigerian who their lovely daughter was sharing a flat with. I spent a lot of time that weekend chatting with her parents whom I would like to believe left Kent with a different impression about Nigerians. In the end, I do not hold anything against my former flat mate's parents for their reaction; because their response was based on the impression the media had fed them about my country all their lives.

The onus rests with the media from developing countries (not just Africa) to deconstruct erroneous imageries by rebranding their countries and correcting these wrong impressions, otherwise they will continue to be misunderstood by the developed world, allowing racism and all the accompanying negative stereotypes to remain a part of life well into the future.

CHAPTER 8

CONCLUSION

I n the preceding five chapters, I have elaborated on five key areas people from developing nations, Africans in particular, both those from the developing countries and those in the diaspora, need to focus their energies and continue to work on, to accelerate economic growth of the continent. In so doing, Africa will reverse the racism she suffers at the hands of those that culturally sanction it. They are my thoughts on what a *multifarious strategy* for emancipating the exploited colored people of the world should look like.

Following the introductory chapters on the causes of racist behavior, chapter three started with the need for increased productivity, because without boosting productivity, it is impossible to industrialize. We then moved on to chapter four where we focused on the all-important role leadership must play across every fabric of society to deliver this much sort after prosperity. After tackling these two main fundamentals, chapter five stresses the need to patronize home grown national products and services offered by national companies from the continent. This is no time to be selling the continent short in an effort to meet *Open Market and Free Trade* obligations established by developed nations far more industrialized than we are. Chapters six and seven go on to expound on the need for more diaspora investment in Africa and then Africans seizing the narrative by rebranding the continent and telling her own story.

Let us summarize these chapters in bullet points as follows;

Productivity
Leadership
African-made products and services
New diaspora investment, and
Tell your African story

Before making my next point, I must mention how at times, I am tempted to chuckle when I hear atheists in the ideological west (which includes western nations not necessarily located in the western hemisphere like Australia, New Zealand etc.) complain about the negative influence Christianity continues to have in their national affairs, when in reality they owe so much of their nations' constitutions to Christendom. As much as it is important to separate religion from matters of state, they need to acknowledge that the very tenets of capitalism, down to more socialists' elements of their constitutions such as the Welfare state, are firmly rooted in Judaist and Christian doctrines. So, it is with that thought in mind that I quote another Bible text relevant to my next point, from the book of Habakkuk 2:2 (NKJV), *"Write the vision and make it plain on tablets, that he may run who reads it."* I am yet to come across a better BC era argument for corporate mission statements than the preceding Bible verse.

Observe how the first letters of each chapter's summary word-phrase above line up nicely to form the acronym P.L.A.N.T. Incidentally, leaders of multi-national corporations involved in strategy development for their organizations will tell you that –when developing guiding principles and values for deployment in big organizations, it is advisable not to exceed a number that can be counted on the digits of one hand. In other words, when the number of points exceeds five, people may struggle to remember all of them. This makes my five-point agenda practical, realistic and easy to remember. The list is by no means exhaustive, you could make an argument for the inclusion of a few more areas or split of some listed areas, but these five in my opinion represent what developing countries like those in Africa can adopt as a pan-African agenda, to galvanize the continent in view of the daunting tasks before it and in so doing, Reverse Racism.

There have been some attempts at adopting such an agenda in the past. For example, the former South African President Thabo Mbeki led "progressive African agenda", which was an ambitious plan to integrate the continent into the global economy on the basis of "mutual responsibility" and "mutual accountability". This might have been a tall order bearing in mind the kinds of fundamental issues that still plagues much of the continent. It also recommended some shared democratic principles on peace and security as the cornerstones of development in Africa, which would have been ideal for the level of development on the continent; with several African nations still struggling with internal strife and trying to achieve social cohesion within their states.

What is needed is for more work to be done on the rudimentary issues I have enumerated here, with more focus in the so-called giants of the continent who boast of the largest populations, including, Nigeria, Ethiopia, Egypt, DR Congo, Tanzania, South Africa and Kenya. Due to the strategic locations of these nations and their size, their prosperity tends to have knock-on effects on neighboring countries in their respective sub-regions within the continent. As discussed in chapter three, they can serve as the *lead* countries in their regions in the "flying geese" model of development, where a "lead" country (not unlike Japan) creates a slipstream for others to follow.

People of African descent world-wide need to avoid being drawn into a pity party or, worse still, getting overcome with bitterness; believing everything we endure in our societies as regards being on the receiving end of discrimination is everyone else's fault except ours. I mentioned earlier that some black folk maybe offended by this, but the truth must be told. We cannot continue to be the people that everyone else uses to feel good about themselves. We should not be predisposed to receiving handouts and accepting the resultant unfair treatment as a people. We need to literally dig ourselves out of this hole sooner rather than later. Today's and future generations of Africans need to *PLANT* the continent back into reckoning in global affairs.

This PLANT acronym reminds me of an old Greek Proverb I stumbled upon about a decade ago which goes something like this;

"A society grows great when old men *plant* trees whose shade they know they shall never sit in."

It is, therefore time old African men began *planting* trees for their unborn children.

By now it should be obvious that I am an advocate for Pan-Africanism. For people, not familiar with the term, Wikipedia defined Pan-Africanism as a "worldwide intellectual movement that aims to encourage and strengthen bonds of solidarity between all people of African descent... It is based on the belief that unity is vital to economic, social, and political progress and aims to "unify and uplift" people of African descent". Readers who may not be conversant with the movement can reference the works and lives of great Pan-Africans such as, Haile Selassie of Ethiopia, Julius Nyerere of Tanzania, Ahmed Sekou Toure of Guinea, Kwame Nkrumah of Ghana, Thomas Sankara of Burkina Faso, Nnamdi Azikiwe of Nigeria and Muammar Gaddafi of Libya. Yes, you read right, Muammar Gaddafi was a Pan-African.

Let us not forget those Pan-Africans from the West such as Marcus Garvey, Malcolm X and academics like W. E. B. Du Bois. An all-African global alliance of sorts is the only way to empower the continent and in so doing, roll back this global scourge called racism.

Pan-Africanism, at its inception was more than just a search for racial or geographic identity. Initially led and popularized by Africans in the diaspora such as Marcus Garvey and W.E.B. DuBois, it was a clear rejection of the laughable fallacy that Africans did not have a history. It was also a strong refutation of the mindset that defined Africa and Africans from the perspective of the historical experience of slavery, colonialism and racial discrimination. Rather, it was the affirmation of the rich cultural heritage of African societies and the importance of achieving freedom and continental unity (Lopes 2013).

Pan-Africanism is in no way new, in fact the legislative arm of the African Union (AU) is called the Pan-African Parliament or African Parliament, located in the South African town of Midrand – a town I have had the pleasure of doing some work in between 2014 and 2016. Like most legislative organizations, I worry that over time politics and bureaucracy may have doused the fire lit by the fore mentioned founding fathers of Pan-Africanism and there is need to rekindle and redefine the movement. I will be the first to admit that social media has provided an avenue for some passionate activists to express themselves to an audience. However, a few of those I have found online appear quite bitter and retributionist, which should not be the foundation of any Pan-African Renaissance. This is because any foundation that does not address the gaps in African society will not even get off the ground, much less yield any result.

The objective should be more about using a roadmap which I have begun to layout in this book to forge a way forward, as opposed to starting off by seeking compensation for past injustices. The honest reason being, even if Africa suddenly got paid a huge reparation settlement right now, it would mostly end up in the pockets of a select few, if the fundamentals highlighted herein are not addressed, and that has been my position for a while. I know this because I continue to see this happen in my country till this day; funds meant for the neediest in society have found their way into private pockets, such that more agencies and non-governmental relief organizations looking for key projects that have the most impact on poor masses, now fund them directly. It is a pity that people can still make a living by conceiving ways to make money off the sufferings of others. Hence, my preference for a Mandela approach and not a Mugabe approach to solving the continents problems. I am not entirely at odds with these online activists; to a large extent like I, they are driven by a need to see people of color treated with equity in society. While I agree with this one hundred percent, I would like to see this accompanied by some genuine economic emancipation to truly enshrine our civil liberties.

By and large after the forays of the former African gladiators, Pan-African activism seems to have hit an unexplainable lull. I am not one to speculate, but I find it strange that none of the Pan-Africans I have listed earlier was a darling of the West. Not only that; some of them either got dramatically ousted from political relevance or met their untimely demise under what can only be described as *mysterious circumstances. Is there something more to this Pan-Africanism that people of African descent in this day and age have failed to see?*

It goes without saying that because of the long-term commitment needed to fix foundational matters of this nature, it only makes sense that the African youth should be the focal point of any renewed efforts; as the mind of the youth remains the battleground of the future.

In Africa, the number of youths is growing rapidly. In 2015, 226 million youth aged 15 – 24 lived in Africa, accounting for 19 percent of the global youth population. By 2030, it is projected that the number of youths in Africa will have increased to 42 percent. Africa's youth population is expected to continue to grow throughout the remainder of the twenty first century, more than doubling from current levels by 2055 (UN ESA 2015). The size of youth population as a percentage of total population seems to have peaked in all regions of the world except Africa. Hence this important and dynamic segment of the population must be the prime focus of reversing the socio-economic fortunes of the continent, regardless of whatever pre-existing cultural barriers that may hold back empowering the youths of Africa.

Across the continent youth are stepping forward in more numbers no longer content to remain part of the audience in governance but now demanding to be more involved. Youths are no longer content to leave their collective destinies in the hands of the elders by letting them continue to decide the continent's fate, especially considering that these elders have not exactly done a marvelous job so far. What youth everywhere need is for their leaders to create a conducive atmosphere for them to express their innate creative energies. As predicted by President Kennedy (see chapter four), they are coming to the realization that if they continue to slumber, their potentials will continue to be stifled.

In the end, we all – both young and old – are members of one society, working towards common goals of progress, preservation of life, welfare and freedom for all its members. With each member doing his or her own part, the society will move toward a desired end. Therefore, every member of society is equally as important and needs to sign on to a Pan-African renaissance that will bring prosperity to the continent and in time, respect will follow.

Some readers, especially non-African readers may see this book as dwelling predominantly on the black experience and less on other races who also endure racism, and they are indeed correct. There are two reasons for this. Firstly, I am African, and it is easy for me to write on this subject based on my perception and experiences on the matter, and without co-writing with some one of another ethnicity or race; I run the risk of misinterpreting and misreporting their opinions on what is a highly sensitive subject. Hence, my decision to play safe and restrict myself to what I believe is more of an African view on the matter, with a corresponding approach to reversing this anomaly.

The second and more important reason I chose to restrict myself to the African perspective is the fact that no other ethnic group or race has suffered and continues to suffer more stigmatization than the Negro. Centuries of a maligning racist agenda has portrayed the skin tone of the Negro as a stigma to the point that, some blacks have come to believe these untruths. The stigma is so deeply engrained that some blacks do everything within their power not to appear black, in terms of mannerism and even their appearance. I believe the choice to stigmatize the Negro was born, more out of the extreme difference in skin pigmentation compared with the early Caucasian visitors to the continent, than anything else (they chose to despise rather than embrace what they did not understand). So, by writing from an African perspective, it is safe to say that I have captured most of the problems plaguing other peoples of color and ethnicities who endure racism in one way or the other.

Also, I will be the first to admit that you may find that some of these five opportunity areas may not apply to your societies. Asians, for instance, have little or no problems with productivity, while patronage of national products and indigenous investment may not be a problem Arabs might struggle with. But most persons from developing countries should be able to relate to some issues highlighted in this book. These afore listed challenges and action plans apply as much to your societies as they do to African communities.

On the other hand, while Africa and the developing world continue this journey towards economic and social emancipation, it is very important that people from developed countries on their part, do their utmost best not to rub salt on sore wounds by continuing to condone and encourage racist rhetoric even in the most private of conversations. As mentioned severally prejudices are not innate, but socially acquired. They need to stay the course and understand that centuries of unfair treatment and exploitation of colored people will not be reversed overnight. There is a similitude between the attitude that underdeveloped nations get from developed ones and the way continental Europe (then called Barbarians) was subjugated by the then Roman Empire just millennia ago. This should be a sign that even this era of underdevelopment in Africa and the rest of the third world, shall pass.

The ideological West need to understand that the current illegal immigration crises with frontlines in the Mediterranean and US-Mexico border can only be resolved if the standards of living in underdeveloped nations improve to the point that illegal migration becomes less attractive. The West needs to pay less lip service and do their part in helping these fledging nations improve their economies. Apart from more capital-intensive efforts like foreign direct investment into these economies, they can start doing the simpler things like ensuring their national corporations doing business in these markets pay correct taxes and are themselves not contributing to the endemic corruption problems in these nations. The United States sets a great example in this regard with its Foreign Corrupt Practices Act and similar legislation which have made US corporations the most tax compliant and torch bearers in the fight against corruption in developing economies.

The West must also do more to discourage corrupt leaders from using their financial institutions as havens for looted funds. Western leaders need to measure their utterances and continue to lead by example by not encouraging, much less, using derogatory language on minorities. Societal barriers notwithstanding, the West must do more by accommodating and being more tolerant of minorities in their societies rather than discriminating against them. This should not be misunderstood as a solicitation for more open borders, but rather an appeal for those minorities who are already legitimate members of their societies to be given the respect that they are entitled to, as fellow human beings and citizens. The West (and East) must continue to encourage inclusion and be less judgmental of minority communities in their countries. Minorities should be made to see that "we are all in," and not have to clamor for their rights. This way, a stronger sense of community and our common humanity can be reaffirmed and preserved. A former Secretary General of the United Nations and a great African, the late Kofi Anan was quoted as saying, "Ignorance and prejudice are the handmaidens of propaganda. Our mission, therefore, is to confront ignorance with knowledge, bigotry with tolerance, and isolation with the outstretched hand of generosity. Racism can, will, and must be defeated."

The capacity to rid our world of racism lies within us all; to quote an old Egyptian saying, "the Kingdom of Heaven is within you, and whosoever shall know himself shall find it". All major religions of the world preach a similar creed; the Bible for instance says in Luke 17:21 (NKJV), "For indeed, the Kingdom of God is within you". Therefore, regardless of our education, social status, family appellation, ethnicity, race or by what name we call God, we all have it within us to accomplish whatsoever we set our minds and hearts to achieve, and that includes stamping out racism, *permanently*.

Final quote,

> **"The best way to predict the future is to create it."**

Divine Bradley

REFERENCES

Anabel Gonzalez, March 2017: "3 challenges Latin American economies must overcome to boost intraregional trade". A World Bank, International Bank of Reconstruction and Development – International Development Association (IBRD-IDA) Report. *worldbank.org*

Carlos Lopes, May 2013: "Moving from early Pan-Africanism towards an African Renaissance," Speech during the AU 50th anniversary in Addis Ababa. *uneca.org*

Dinfin Mulupi, January 2015: "Six emerging real estate investment hotspots in Africa", *howwemadeitinafrica.com*

Dr. Manisha Kumari Deep, 2018: "The Way of Prime Minister Narendra Modi's Leadership," *grin.com*

Dr. Mimi Cowan, 2013: "Irish-America and the 1916 Rising." *rte.ie*

Dylan Matthews, July 2014: "A Central America expert explains the root causes of the migrant crisis," an interview with Cynthia Arnson (Director of the Latin American Program at the Woodrow Wilson International Center for Scholars). *vox.com*

H. A. Wieschhoff, 1941: "The Social Significance of Names Among the Ibo of Nigeria", page 212. *anthrosource.onlinelibrary. wiley.com*

H. Shroff, 2018: "Skin Color, Cultural Capital, and Beauty Products: An Investigation of the Use of Skin Fairness Products in Mumbai, India", US National Library of Medicine National Institutes of Health. *ncbi.nlm.nih.gov*

John-Paul Iwuoha, March 1, 2017: "5 Exciting Reasons Why You Should Start A Business in Africa's Agribusiness Industry … NOW!" *smallstarter.com*

Jane H. Hill, 2008: "The Everyday Language of White Racism," page 9.

Jessica Faieta, March 2017: "Challenges and opportunities for Latin America and the Caribbean in 2017." *undp.org*

Kurt Davis, June 2015: "Five African Countries That Offer the Greatest Investment Opportunities in Real Estate," *venturesafrica.com*

Manny Otiko, May 15, 2015: "African Americans Are Finding Success in Africa's Tech Gold Rush, So Can You", *atlantablackstar.com*

Michael Camilleri and Ben Raderstorf, January 2018: "*Latin America's Unusual Leadership Vacuum.*" Americas Quarterly.

Michael Harriot, October 2017: "Why We Never Talk About Black-on-Black Crime: An Answer to White America's Most Pressing Question." *theroot.com*

Nadra Kareem Nittle, Aug. 6, 2017: "Understanding 4 different Types of Racism" *ThoughtCo.com*

Philip Bump, October 2017: "America's big issue is 'black Africans' killing each other, Sebastian Gorka says." *washingtonpost.com*

Study Moose, August 2016: "The influence of media on society Essay", page 9, *studymoose.com*

Teun A. van Dijk, 2012: "The Role of the Press in the Reproduction of Racism," page 17 *springer.com*

The Economist, Nov 7, 2015: "There is a long road ahead for Africa to emulate East Asia." *economist.com*

References

The Slasher Pastor blog, 2016: "Healing the wounds of racism through Jesus and His Church: Notes from the Church Ministries Conference." *slasherpastor.wordpress.com*

UN Department of Economic and Social Affairs, May 2015: "Youth population trends and sustainable development." *un.org/esa*

Victor Adeyemi 2017: "Servant Leadership", Harvest House Publishing, page 10.

Whitehead, Talahite and Moodley, 2013: "Gender and Identity", Oxford University Press, pg. 67.

18 Karat Reggae, 2017: "Interracial children are more beautiful than Black children, according to Kanye West." *18karatreggae.com*